JOHN ELLSWORTH WINTER

John Ellsworth Winter

UNDOOMED WARRIOR

THE STRANGE CASE OF R. E. LEE
AND THE "GETTYSBURG" CAMPAIGN

*Wyrd oft nered
Unfaegne eorl
ponne his ellen deah*

*"Fate often nutures
Undoomed the warrior
When his courage endures."*

Beowulf 571

**Cadmus House
Harrisburg, PA**

Undoomed Warrior
The Strange Case of R. E. Lee and the "Gettysburg" Campaign
All Rights Reserved.
Copyright © 2013 John Ellsworth Winter, (jellsworthw@comcast.net)
v4.0

Cadmus House (cadmushouse1@gmail.com)

ISBN: 978-0-578-11575-7

Library of Congress Control Number: 2012952606

PRINTED IN THE UNITED STATES OF AMERICA

For Elva Joan

✧✧✧

We needs must love the highest when we see it.
Alfred, Lord Tennyson

CORRIGENDA

P. 82   Para. 3, Line 4, spelling
                "Eire" should be "Erie"
P. 168, Para. 2, Line 6, spelling:
                "aggresion" should be "aggression"
P. 175, Para. 5, Line, 4, dating:
                "1780" should be "1870"
P. 181, Para. 2, Line 1, spelling:
                "To may" should be "Too many"
P. 194, Para.1, Line 5, naming:
                "Christ" should be "St. Paul's"

Contents

Why did Lee march into Pennsylvania?
You think you know?
Think again.

Examining startling facts
Professor John Ellsworth Winter, Ph.D., lights up the events leading to the Battle of Gettysburg.

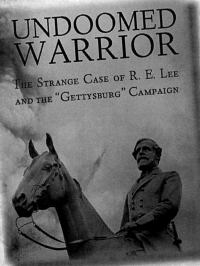

Here's a little taste: As early as 8 September 1862 R. E. Lee asked that a "proposal of peace" be sent to the North. Documented in official records, his letter to Jefferson Davis, months before the battle at Gettysburg, shows him to be a peace—seeker. Davis refused. The war dragged on. Additional information from within the Confederate War Office 30 June 1863 … 5 P.M. to be exact … states that General Lee actually went to Pennsylvania not to fight, *"but proclaim to the inhabitants that all we desire is PEACE, not conquest."*

What happened to that *"wisest, grandest, most imposing"* plan? How did Lee find himself entangled in Gettysburg — the great disaster of his career?

Please join Dr. Winter for a free presentation and discussion of his book, *Undoomed Warrior: The Strange Case of R. E. Lee and The "Gettysburg" Campaign* (Harrisburg: Cadmus House, 2013).

~ *SPEAKING/BOOK SIGNINGS* ~
AMERICAN CIVIL WAR MUSEUM COMPLEX
297 Steinwehr Ave., Gettysburg
Sunday, 30 June 2013, 11 AM — 1 PM, tent;
Tuesday, 2 July, 11 AM — 1 PM, tent • Wednesday, 3 July, 11 AM — 1 PM, tent;
Thursday, 4 July, 3 — 5 PM; inside, signing • Friday, 5 July, 1 — 3 PM, tent;
Saturday, 6 July, 11 AM — 1 PM, tent • Sunday, 7 July, 11 AM — 1 PM, tent.

TRINITY UNITED CHURCH OF CHRIST, 60 East High St., Gettysburg
Wednesday Evening, 26 June 2013, 7 PM Extended presentation, Q & A; signing.

UNITED METHODIST CHURCH, 30 West High St., Gettysburg
Tuesday Evening, 2 July 2013, 7 PM
Extended presentation, Q & A; signing. Parking in rear lot.

CHAPTER 1

"Minute and Precious Particles"

EVIDENCE DOESN'T EXIST that R. E. Lee planned to do battle at Gettysburg. In fact he was aiming elsewhere, to do something strange, something approaching unbelievable.

His plan became a goal-too-far at the ridges and fields, rocks and farmland of Gettysburg. Sometime United States Army War College and West Point historian Dr. Carol Reardon affirms, *"Lee's Army of Northern Virginia had been victorious at the battle called Chancellorsville in May of 1863. They're taking advantage of their victory to march north into Pennsylvania. We're not entirely sure why Lee decides to move north ... Nobody planned to fight at Gettysburg."*[1]

We can scratch Gettysburg as Lee's goal. Point-blank: There never was a campaign as such for Gettysburg. It was an accidental battle --- and R. E. Lee did not plan accidents.

Only a very few ... if that nanonumber ... knew what he was drawing a bead on: A higher goal. Elsewhere!

The issues of where and why Lee was going northward in the summer of 1863 have been unresolved for a century and a half. However, the issues are not irresolvable.

After the war the best-selling *Barnes History of the United States* was used as a textbook in schools of all of the re-united states. Written by former Union Captain Joel Steele, it openly acknowledged the bravery of many Southern troops and their families as equal to the bravery of Northern soldiers and loved ones. That extraordinary quality of bravery found in ordinary people—sparsely noted by the re-tellers of history as military accomplishments or failures—had compelled Steele to tell the truth about valor, Northern and Southern, even though some Northerners complained about his honesty.

In fact, Steele's stories of the bravery of ordinary people warranted a commendation about that much-veiled value, which came through on the half-title page of his next successful *History of Ancient Peoples*: *"Truth comes down to us from the past, as gold is washed down in the mountains of the Sierra Nevada, in minute and precious particles."*

Much history is undocumented story telling about such particles. If we want to make sense of it we have to fill in blanks, connect dots, so to speak.

Connecting the dots is what our physical senses do. No single sense, nor even all five, can give a complete story of anything. Each physical sense perceives or receives only a certain number of angstrom units on the electromagnetic scale of reality. Thus each sense perceives a story in partial pieces, incomplete chunks, and fragmentary tidbits that we intellectually glue together to make sense of what has gone on prior to us and is going on around us in the Present.

Thoughtful people realize that the Past never has been an adequate carrier of itself into the Present. Prime Minister Winston Churchill characterized that plight succinctly when addressing the British House of Commons on 12 November 1940 in World War II: *"History with its flickering lamp stumbles along the trail of the past, trying to reconstruct its scenes, to revive its echoes, and kindle with pale gleams the passion of former days."*

As a consequence, we have to struggle to search, find, and extract *particles* from the Past, much as gold particles are extracted from the richest-ever American gold mine. In the Carlin Trend area of northeastern Nevada new deposit sites still are being opened in the twenty-first century. There, interestingly, the element AU—number 79 on the Periodic Table of the physical elements, namely gold, precious gold—cannot be detected by the naked eye. Yet it can be detected *microscopically.* Factually, more gold is unearthed today by such pit mining than by any other method in all of human history.

History, too, needs to dig, intellectually, for microscopic particles around us. It should not repeat only the already-told story lines. History is obliged to dig elsewhere ... everywhere ... for minute particles that have come down, and are coming down.

Such a precious particle was discovered quite recently, in May 2012, concerning Abraham Lincoln. Although not part of the Lee story, it shows how precious particles of historical gold come down to us.

Dr. Charles Leale, a Northern army physician had been in attendance at Ford's Theater in Washington, about 40 feet away from Lincoln when the assassin shot the President from behind on 14 April 1865. Dr. Leale rushed to the presidential box and sought to help President Lincoln, who was in a comatose state, severely wounded and totally unresponsive. The physician thought the President had been stabbed because John Wilkes Booth had a dagger in his hand when he jumped to the stage shouting an ancient curse on President Lincoln. The young physician inadvertently discovered with his left little finger that there was a clean round hole in the President's skull and then knew he had been shot. When he withdrew his finger blood began to ooze from the hole and the President seemed to respond. Dr. Leale ordered the body taken to a house across the street from the theater.

Dr. Leale wrote his clinical report the next day. That report lay in the National Archives in Washington for almost a century and a half among the papers of the U. S. Army's surgeons general until found by a staff researcher 21 May 2012. The report is minute, precious particle about an historical event.

That same May day, Tom Siegfried, Editor-in-Chief of *Science News* published an editorial "Scientific advances stem from surprises in the past." He indicated science is open to all kinds of evidence: "Taking note of surprising phenomena is the first step toward making great discoveries." Fresh material enhances the quest for reality; surprising phenomena are still to be found in history, making for significant discoveries.

Science, for example, is open to all kinds of evidence; fresh material enhances its quest for reality. *"Scientific advances stem from surprises in the past ... Taking note of surprising phenomena is the first step toward making great discoveries."*[2] And, *"Current science at its best demonstrates how the science of the past wasn't the whole story."*[3] There's no question but that self-correction is the strong point of science, readiness to revise its judgments in the face of fresh evidence. History is prone to hold its positions religiously: "What I have written I have written." Rather, it would do well to emulate its sister-study's readiness to revise its judgment with fresh evidence that lay bare more pieces of information.

Literally, minute and precious particles of historical gold—some nugget sized—have come to us and can help resolve the strange issues of why and where General Robert Edward Lee led the Army of Northern Virginia in June-July of 1863 in its Northern Campaign.

Not the stuff of legend and grandeur, some particles, often obscure—*or obscured!*—of the rationale behind the Southern invasion of the North, are passed over easily. They are mundane records seemingly with no or little historical worth. Seeming unconnected to similar mundane records, these particles thus go purposely unnoted, unplaced, even spurned because minute.

Nonetheless, they're frequently immense in value, "golden." Certainly they're not just intellectual tailings, garbage. When joined to one another, regardless of smallish proportions, they have incremental meanings all their own that can make solid steps toward discoveries in history. There is still more truth to break forth ... from unnoted history, history known but not considered worthy of note or application.

We benefit from these precious particles, for truth demands consideration of all sources. The declaration, *"Those who cannot remember the past are condemned to repeat it,"*[4] is accepted by the vast majority of historians and was propounded by the Harvard philosopher George Santayana. Just as importantly he stated, *"History is always written wrong, and so always needs to be re-written."*[5] Minute particles from the Past mined in the present can help get the rewrite of history right.

True, historians have a ponderous task. A task not to be envied, for *Everything* rushes at them. Minute and precious particles can be missed easily as historians deal with *all* from the Past they can lay their hands on. They filter, extract what is meaningful to them, yet obviously do not catch all particles. They judge some particles as void of historical significance. They choose which stories to tell—and therein lies the rub.

Yet precious other particles do exist, some critical to a fuller understanding of the Past. Literally treasures, those outwardly inconsequential or "missing" particles, in certain instances, can change prevailing history as construed by popular assumptions. Again, Santayana provides guidance by stressing a crucial contrary: *"The function of history ... is not passively to reproduce its subject-matter."*[6] Historians leave gaps in the Past, many because minute particles are put in bottom drawers, missed, or even discarded totally.

No matter how many books are written about past leaders, how many studies are done, there are still more breaking forth. Abraham Lincoln is a prime example of a leader who is ever emerging out of American history. R. E. Lee keeps emerging as well. The boundaries of Lee's life, career, and thought remain open, inviting new approaches, new ideas, and new interpretations rather than passive reproduction of received traditions. Precious particles, minute traces: There are more to come about R. E. Lee.

Lee was more practical than we image because he was close to scores of important people from whom he heard much. Yet he was closer, crucially closer, to thousands upon thousands of ordinary men, living what they lived, sleeping on bare earth, eating cabbage too often, under constant threat of death during days of foot-slogging, soul-searching monotony punctuated with a few marvelous days, and visibly—after age 46—always thankful, publicly or privately, to God to be alive.

Lee was more imaginative than we want him to be in our pre-conceived ideas of the military master we've been told he was. And he was more committed to the Southern cause than we have thought—though he finally became un-committed when through its *defeat* he realized the cause had come shockingly close to destroying the magnificent American experiment begun in 1776. As a consequence he became more committed to the United States of America than his adorers understood, making it his *modus operandi* while, as "President Lee of Washington College," he helped his students to be Southern, and American, and Christian.

R. E. Lee came to realize in his forties that the flow of his life had a religious undercurrent; Christian in essence, but fairly non-denominational, non-theological, certainly non-dogmatic in practice. He and his young male students were moving to a grander tune for a vaster purpose than personal success, or defeat of enemies, or attainment of fame.

In character and communication Lee made evident that he was committed to virtue rather than victory, to rectitude rather than winning. He was also more dedicated to a better political state than to a tribal-style government, that is, a government ruling from the heights of privilege and elitism. He was dedicated to a government more in tune with a community of people searching and striving to live under God's guidance, rather than dedicated to a people thinking and acting as if they and their government *already* had that blessing bestowed on them, esteeming others as lesser beings without God's guidance.

Lee's public demeanor when college president showed his true colors. In joint exercises at holidays, his Washington College students paraded through Lexington, Virginia, with the Virginia Military Institute cadets; but Lee never wore a military uniform nor insignia. And each time, he purposely marched out of step! Also, he purposely put an end to both research and writing about the war. He sharply opposed any unfavorable comments about his great adversary, General Ulysses Grant. Such actions gave strong evidence of a different Lee. It's true he did not forbid students, neighbors, or friends to address him as "General," but he neither encouraged nor initiated the practice. Lee knew he did not command an army. He was *collegianus,* in a partnership with trustees, faculty, students, and parents of students.

He participated quietly in the academic community of scholarly faculty and student "scholars-in-the-making" as a service to Washington College, which served country and God.

In the South R. E. Lee's public hallmark was as a Christian gentleman—except when he was riding through town or countryside and delighted in putting on display his acclaimed horsemanship skills with his "friend" *Traveller.* Vanity at its minimum; a venial sin—if that!

Whether at chapel services or faculty meetings, in curriculum development or receiving students, in public appearances and in religious duties, he influenced others not by imperious efforts but by a stoical and fraternal presence that put them at ease.

Robert Lee lived a piety as close to *hero* or *saint* in the public mind as the piety lived by the nation's other perceived hero, saint, and *martyr,* Abraham Lincoln. South and North—though probably not thoroughly comprehended—were enlarged, even exalted, by two warriors for *peace.* Today, all four … Lee & Lincoln and South & North … are exalted and enlarged, 150 years after the two men lived on opposite sides of the issues of Slavery and Secession as well as the different sides of the Potomac River.

Lee's reversal of military role from training young men to kill to the role of educating young men to *live* for the collective good makes complete sense. Had he done otherwise, along with his young men, the South would have warred on endlessly, perpetually, and relentlessly until "Peace is War" and "War is Peace" would have become their reality. Lee knew his life then would be devoid of meaning, thoroughly unchristian. At its end he chose not to live betwixt and between victories and defeats. Life was too precious to R. E. Lee to end in such a maelstrom, a turbulence of death … his own life, or the lives of his loved ones and enemies, likewise.

Simply put, Robert Edward Lee wanted peace to *reign* rather than victory to *rule*.

Bundled together, some precious particles, tiny nuggets of what one newspaper editor called the *wisest, grandest, and most imposing* plan, extracted from the Past and coming down to us, manifest Lee's very special purpose for his Northern Campaign.

His stature after the wreck of the largest battle of the war, at Gettysburg, continued secure, however, and enlarges in modern times to more than life-size. That magnified stature is rendered unmistakably in the striking statue of R. E. Lee on his charger Traveller at that bloody field of battle, the place where his unique plan collapsed, where the war turned fatal for the Confederacy, and where his reputation became legendary as an "undoomed warrior."

Chapter Notes

1. "Booknotes" C-Span Network with Brian Lamb, 10 December 1997 (http://www.c-spannvideo.org/program/96629-1).
2. Tom Siegfried (Editor in Chief). Science News. 21 May 2011. 2.
3. Ibid., 31 December 2011. 2.
4. George Santayana. (1905). Reason In Common Sense (N.Y.: Scribner's. 1905): 284
5. Santayana. Reason In Science (N.Y.: Scribner's, 1906): 6. (Emphasis added)
6. Santayana. Egotism In German Philosophy (N.Y.: Scribner's, 1916):

CHAPTER 2

"Wisest, Grandest, Most Imposing Scheme"

BOLD TO THE point of recklessness after two unequivocally massive victories, General Robert E. Lee wanted to go for three.

Fredericksburg in December 1862 had been a slugfest. It was a brawl but with bayonets not brassknuckles, cannonballs not clubs, and grapeshot in place of groin kicks.

Chancellorsville in May 1863 was pure surgery, in the sense of its ancient Greek noun *cheirourgia*: "having in hand, pursuing practically." Lee and General "Stonewall" Jackson performed surgery on Federal General Hooker. "Fighting Joe" Hooker became like a postoperative medical patient in a stupor, groaning, "To tell the truth, I just lost confidence in Joe Hooker." The Federal Army of the Potomac, larger and much better provisioned than Lee's, looked futilely weak in action, often on the ropes or usually backpedaling, was unable to win fights or respect … from anyone.

R. E. Lee immediately gained the stature of a master strategist and tactician, like Napoleon Bonaparte or Julius Caesar: one who makes his wrong moves turn out right.

In the victorious process Lee reasoned the Army of Northern Virginia was so exultant—and near to invincible—it could deliver an exceptional knockout blow to end all knockout blows to an enemy who just kept staggering in front of them unable to counterpunch. Emboldened, General Lee planned to confront the Federal enemy a third time, this time to end the war. But with a distinctive, even quirky, quick-footed maneuvering, almost a sparring match style campaign!

Less than two months later everything reversed. The nightmare of a goal within reach—yet receding with every step that his army marched on enemy soil—tormented R. E. Lee. A critical defeat resulted almost unbelievably.

Day One. Fighting of that defeat had started auspiciously for the Confederates on 1 July 1863. In the first round Johnny Reb virtually scored a knockout. The Army of the Potomac backpedaled through Gettysburg, Pennsylvania, then staggered and struggled up Cemetery Hill.

Day Two could be said to have been a draw between the heavyweights, each side earning points with body punches yet neither one falling through the ropes, or decked on the canvas.

Day Three the armies seemed to have clutched one another, throwing hateful uppercuts, bombarding each other. Then a Confederate bull-like charge out in the open ended with the Army of Northern Virginia punch drunk and dying.

All the while the Commanding General sat on a log watching! It would appear that he was waiting for his cavalry commander Jeb Stuart to slip around his Army of Northern Virginia *a la Stonewall Jackson at Chancellorsville* and outflank the Northern Army in order to punch a stealth blow to its back. Stuart's cavalry would attack from the rear at the same time the infantry was staging Pickett's Charge—to defeat. And fame. Lee intended to split apart the Northern defense line by a pincer move.

However, a Michigan Wolverine stymied that action, inadvertently. While passing by three miles east of the main battlefield to go on duty elsewhere, a brash Federal officer and his brave cavalrymen were co-opted from their assignment. They joined a Federal cavalry general's forces in protecting the side and rear of the Federal line. Michiganer George Custer, newly minted Brigadier General, stopped famous Confederate cavalry commander Jeb Stuart in his (horse) tracks on the East Cavalry Field. Lee's infantry assault with Pickett's Charge also failed. The pincer movement failed. The battle at Gettysburg failed. The

Confederacy failed. The Confederate cavalry was fought to a standstill before it could even get close to the Federal line.

Thus the Confederate infantry on the main battlefield charged, unsupported. Pickett and 13,000 men hit the canvas. Lee's Northern Campaign was down for the count.

And Robert E. Lee wondered, "If they had been supported as they were to have been—but, for some reason not yet full explained to me, were not—we would have held the position and the day would have been ours. Too bad. Too bad. Oh, too bad!"[1]

Day Four. Independence Day. The glorious Fourth of July. The great Southern army having lost independence, incapable of duking it out with counterpunches, ducked out in the rain, heading back to Virginia.

The pleasant woods and fertile fields of southcentral Pennsylvania had become death traps and burial grounds instead of victory laps for Southern fighters. That fight materialized as the turning point of the "war to make peace" between the states of the American Republic. As well, it gained an address like no other in all American history.

Lee survived. His plan did not … and vanished from history. R. E. Lee nevertheless remained unfazed. Undoomed.

The abrasive defeat at Gettysburg soon nicked razor-like across the face of Southern self-praise. However, with bravado the editor of the *Richmond Daily Dispatch* on Tuesday, 28 July 1863 had—at the eye-grabbing upper left corner on page one, column one—attacked such Southern dismay. The South had been appalled with its best general's lacerated plan. His army's unforeseen collapse and precarious retreat botched his special plan for invasion of the North. In the face of the public's taunting contempt for the failed effort the editor staunchly supported Lee's unsuccessful plan—to the full. Strange indeed: The editor named Lee's defeated plan, *"one of the wisest, grandest, most imposing schemes ever conceived by the mind of man."* Something about R. E. Lee's plan was startling.

Southerners couldn't help but be anxiety ridden as tension and doubt rampaged through Dixieland. Two opposing ideas had to be made compatible—somehow. From the specific point of view, either Lee was a victor or he was a loser. From the general point of view, either the Confederacy was God-ordained or God had deserted the Confederacy, so they thought.

People had two choices: the specific or the general viewpoint. But many Southerners were deeply disturbed because self-righteously they had assured themselves they were right and blessed by God and therefore didn't have to make a choice. God was on their side: *fait accompli*. Therefore, they didn't have to choose, since God would give them the victory, literally.

On the rational side, other Southerners saw that if they chose the negative phase of either choice—Lee as loser or the Confederacy as God-deserted—the results would destroy their Secession and Rebellion. If they chose the positive phase of either choice—Lee as victor or the Confederacy as God ordained—it was terrifying then to accept that the bad loss at Gettysburg was a good thing or that it was God's plan all along to allow the Federals to win.

Southerners didn't know what to make of the military and political defeat at Gettysburg. Their tribal view of God's involvement in human affairs was primitive and really not Christian to the degree they thought.

Consequently, people in the South didn't know what to make of their religion, either. An office holder in the Confederate War Department wrote on 29 July 1863, after the lost battle, "Is Providence frowning upon us for our sins, or upon our cause?"[2] Two days later he quoted a Confederate senator: "[O]ur recent disasters, and Lee's failure in Pennsylvania have nearly ruined us, and the destruction [will] be complete unless France and England can be induced to interfere in our behalf ... people are fast losing ... Hope."[3] And the loss of religious hope is the loss of religion.

Cognitive dissonance reigned in the South. People took the appeasing "Scarlett O'Hara Pose," feeble as it was: *"After all ... tomorrow is another day."* No wonder it is called "S.O.P.," sop, or

placation, fluff, indulgence, head-in-the-sand. Both cognitive dissonance and appeasement are reckless ways to live the present as it
leans up against the future swiftly approaching.

Chapter Notes

1. Harry Hansen. The Civil War: A History (N.Y.: New American Library, 2001): 403.
2. John Beauchamp Jones. A Rebel War Clerk's Diary At The Confederate States Capital (Phila.: Lippincott, 1866): I. 390.
3. Ibid. I. 391.

CHAPTER 3

Lies Often Told in Silence

A HUSH FELL over the seat of the government of the Confederate States of America in May 1863. Silence reigned during and after the planning sessions for Robert E. Lee's summertime Northern Campaign to invade enemy territory.

It is curious and nearly unbelievable that the first instance of historical gold concerning that campaign is a no-show! Official records of the Southern planning sessions for their Northern Campaign are non-existent. Their "history" is blank.

Absence always tells a story. Often "nothing" is a cover for "there wasn't anything there for Southerners of the time to support or to question." Something truly important must have transpired at the planning sessions.

Even the authorized *Papers of Jefferson Davis* are blank for 14-17 May 1863. Their silence can't be blamed on the supposed destruction of Davis' papers by the fire set to Richmond by Confederates when their troops evacuated the city in 1865. Ambiguity, disappearance, paucity and their like are still a story; they have a reason behind them. Absence of records must have a reason behind it, too. What's not there speaks—under its breath, one might say. Or as a mid-twentieth century lyric stated, "Silence tells me secretly everything ..."

The absence of official records is blatant; one is amazed upon realizing other Davis papers before and after those dates are complete. Although blank about the Northern Campaign plans, Davis' papers abound with minutiae dealing with civilian gripes, demands, and suggestions.

Lee's meetings various times with President Davis, Secretary of War James E. Seddon, Adjutant General (and senior general) of the Confederate Army Samuel Cooper, and members of the Presidential Cabinet—to plan and to approve or reject the Northern Campaign—get nary a note or a scribble. One might think President Davis was asleep for four days in May '63. The major Southern campaign of the war—with its bloodiest battle—does not appear. Davis gave no documentary evidence of what was planned, of its rationale. None.

Documentary evidence in official Confederate War Office papers of the plans to invade the North in 1863 is AWOL. Zilch. No chronicles are known to exist for the Northern Campaign planning anywhere.

Obviously, the defeated general's papers are bare. Who would expect otherwise?

Edwin Coddington, in his sweeping study of *The Gettysburg Campaign,* in Chapter 1, quickly states: *"No minutes were kept—at least none was ever found—so there is no way of knowing exactly what Lee said in favor of his proposal or what questions were asked of him."* Coddington shortly followed it with a statement concerning correspondence between President Davis and General Lee about the meetings: "This exchange is hard to understand and makes one wonder what in fact the two men *did* discuss during Lee's several visits to Richmond."[1] By all appearances Lee didn't document his failed plan, purpose, or place of action. By all appearances nobody documented the failed plan!

After the war was over General Cooper, Adjutant General of the Confederate States Army, turned over records—supposedly complete—to the Federal Government. Nowhere do those records exhibit plans for the South's Northern Campaign by Robert Lee, Jefferson Davis, or Cabinet members. An old proverb from Sophocles says that "Silence is a woman's best garment," but it is far truer of military mistakes.

A Compilation of the Official Records of the Union and Confederate Armies states that "Toward the close of hostilities many papers of great historical value were *intentionally destroyed* by their holders, and a still greater number was *concealed*. ... and in various ways the official Confederate files were depleted."[2] Destroyed! Concealed! Depleted! Intentionally. Silence has a reason behind it, where there are military mistakes, especially.

Whether the records are non-existent by chance, by choice, or by cover-up is unknown. Possibly the May 1863 official planning records simply vanished. Like a ghost? More feasibly something was done with them or to them.

Doubtless the stratagem of the plan went awry up north in Pennsylvania.

It was a stratagem after all. Stratagems, scandalously, are convoluted; they are machinations, ploys, very close to tricks. The failure rate of tricks in warfare is enormously high. And, if the groundwork for the scheme had been done hurriedly—superficially, by its very nature—the failure rate could approach 100 percent.

Lee had only a week or so after the Confederate victory at Chancellorsville to prepare a case to present to his superiors in Richmond. Also, he had little time to prepare the Army of Northern Virginia for its movement northward. It was touch-and-go to get both planning and operations, stirring. Planning may have suffered.

After the Gettysburg debacle there was a need in mid-summer of '63 to justify to Southern governors and officials the purpose behind the spectacular battle at Gettysburg because of its onerous tactical and strategic losses. A mega-need, too, cried out: justification to people all over the South regarding the mountainous three-day death toll of fathers, sons, brothers, husbands, uncles, nephews, and friends.

Justification never was given. People had to swallow defeat and be quiet. Absentee records of the plan that led to defeat had to be accepted by everyone as usual *modus operandi*. And then the fall of Vicksburg, Mississippi at the same time, 4 July 1863, smothered the Southern public in disbelief, and shame.

People didn't want to hear more bad news such as poor planning and faulty leadership, especially by R. E. Lee—victorious, glorious, God-given Robert Edward Lee—who had two gigantic victories to his name. Lieutenant General John Pemberton out west at Vicksburg was another story entirely. Because he surrendered Vicksburg, he was castigated severely by many outside and inside the Confederate States Army for one reason: he was a Northerner. Pemberton had accepted the Southern cause yet many thought him a traitor. He served loyally, but couldn't win Southern approval.

Revealing the purpose of Lee's plan supposedly could have met both home-front needs: satisfying government officials and soothing the public's pain. More likely, the facts of questionable planning would have consternated states' officials, and would have amplified the emotional trauma of mothers, daughters, sisters, wives, aunts, nieces, and friends across the South.

So a decision for the planning records to fade away seems to have been not only doable but also helpful. Why upset people with evidence of debatable plans? Sub-par planning could reek of the leaders' pride, a deadly sin if ever there were one. And the purpose of the plan would have been extremely suspect, especially if it was esoteric and seemingly non-martial, non-aggressive, "no general battle intended."

The likelihood of expungement of the records, therefore, remains real. Blotting out the records would hide the multitude of assumptions and the delusion of invincibility. Planning session records would have had to disappear.

The South was in confusion after Gettysburg; misbelief blanketed the Confederate nation. Rational Southerners were obliged to call into question their own usage of the disparaging sobriquets "Invaders" and "Aggressors" to describe Northerners. They, too, had become invaders, aggressors. Although beaten back, their soldiers nonetheless had been invaders. Phrases such as the war of "Northern Aggression" and war of "Northern Invasion" still echoed throughout Dixie, but the words fell ill-suited, even shameful when uttered because the Southern army had done the same thing; two wrongs never make a right, even in warfare.

At first the South had thought the North should get a taste of its own medicine by invasion. *"Tit for tat"* became a facile indictment on Southern tongues before the public learned that Lee was repulsed at Gettysburg. After defeat their collective consciousness had to swallow the idiom, and swallow it whole: *"Tit for tat. You kill my dog, I'll kill your cat!"* That supposed wisdom became a bitter pill, ultimately sickening them because it had to be re-swallowed time and again. The North continued marching through Dixieland, toward the sea, the mountains, the lowlands, swamps, cotton fields, the tobacco roads. Swallowing one's own medicine is a nasty treatment.

Then Vicksburg, Mississippi fell to Major General Ulysses Grant. It was the same day that Lee started units back to Virginia. The Confederate house of cards was starting to fall on, of all days, the Fourth of July! Independence Day, the all-American national day celebrated both north and south of the Mason-Dixon Line. It was the very day that Southerners—not knowing of Lee's intention for peace—wanted to rejoice in his victory announcement up north in Pennsylvania. Their hope for subsequent independence from the North fell flat, conceivably not to stand again.

Why has not the significance of a relationship between our greatest non-religious national holiday and the 1863 invasion plans by the South bestirred writers? Is it because the lost hope for independence, freedom of most every kind, is to Americans—south, north, east, west—so depressing that it obliterates many attendant facts and attitudes?

Independence is such a massive human desire, and a day of its remembrance so powerful and joyous, that much is subservient to their power. Would not an intellect as sharp as Lee's, would not a heart nurtured for independence in his family's Revolutionary War history, would not a *habitus*—a disposition, a character—of duty trained at West Point to protect independence, would not those points have emphasized, collectively and markedly, Independence Day for a sensational, breathtaking attempt to end a divisive war? Was the Fourth of July so insignificant that Lee would miss it?

The loss of that initiative for the Fourth of July caused Lee existential loss. It is of little wonder that five weeks later, 8 August 1863, when his army was safe, comparatively speaking, he wrote to President Davis proffering his resignation, parroting his resignation from the United States Army in 1861 at the start of Secession. His *"wisest, grandest, most imposing scheme"* had failed; he thought he might not be up to further initiatives. As a daily reader of the Bible, Lee could have seen clearly the ghostly fingers without a hand writing on the wall of the book of Daniel: MENE, MENE, TEKEL, u-PHARSIN: "Your days are numbered, you've been weighed on the scales and found wanting, and your enemies will divide and conquer." He knew Scripture well; its implications very well.

Since 1863, dependable scholars and buffs have either bypassed the issues of the planning and purpose of the Northern Campaign— the why and wherefore, the rationale and objective—or they have been frustrated by the lack of official documentation.

Naturally then, portrayals of the whole campaign into Pennsylvania have turned unrealistically from defeat, retreat, attempted resignation, to something that would be an impressive substitute. A super-abundantly recorded defeat-event does well to turn away from reality.

The battle at Gettysburg itself, spectacular, well recorded, and like nothing else in American history for either Southerners or Northerners, would cover up a whole host of sins. It was spectacular; so impressive that it would provide cover to sound off with stories of Southern bravery, such as so-called Pickett's Charge, equaling the Charge of the Light Brigade that British invaders executed against the Russians nine years before and disastrously, of course. But when one is covering up failure, nothing succeeds like spectacle. Or the purported malfeasance of General Longstreet, shifting the blame to one's own, rather than acknowledging that the enemy "had something to do with it," as General Pickett said after the war. Nothing succeeds like implying a traitor within the ranks who caused the loss, rather than giving credit to the victor. The South told itself that failure, and death in a failure, are good. Bragging is a collective illness that only time might help forget, not heal.

Clearly the Battle of Gettysburg is the triumph of spectacle over rationality. The exultation of a sensational event over *the reason for it* is easy, whereas the reason for most every human event is difficult to discern—and the greater the event the more complex its reasons. Gettysburg was gargantuan. It quickly became an end in itself for its chroniclers and interpreters. Clarifying the context in which it occurred, that is, the rationale for which R. E. Lee launched the Northern Campaign, ceased being interesting.

The spectacular battle amounted to an overthrow of reason—the conquest of purpose by phenomenon. Battlefields are vivid and lurid phenomena; multiple deaths always are. Gettysburg was—and still is—a red-hot event, one truly without precise beginning, *sans* planning record. And its ending, too, is red-hot. The "Battle of Gettysburg" was too big to fail! For either combatant.

It still is too big to fail. More Americans visit that battlefield than any other. They tend to think of the battle as an end in itself: the be-all and end-all of Secession and Rebellion. And, since it happened at such a lovely place, it leaves some visitors feeling warm and fuzzy all over. Emotion easily overcomes facts on the ground.

The upshot is that much truth of why the Battle of Gettysburg happened is barely known. If known, the truth is not well acknowledged. Who seeks the "why" when the battle was so spectacular? It's not unusual that "spectacular trumps truth." It happens often in Hollywood. Nightly on television. And every so often in history the truth is obscured by exhibition. Then follows the telling of history with a spin, with a pre-judgment that big is better than anything else.

Thankfully, there is valid history beyond truant planning records. Beyond even flashy combat zones, especially those that have the carnage cleared away, the killing fields manicured, the impressive monuments all in a row, knowledgeable guides, beautiful scenery—and clean restrooms.

Evidence does exist in minute and precious particles from various sources, some of which confirm the strange rationale Lee was using on his invasion northward, going "elsewhere" for a special purpose, on the patriotic day of days in America.

Almost a secret hidden in plain sight, the story comes down to us in priceless pieces that we can find, recognize, and solidify into an answer. It summons out of the silence.

Chapter Notes

1. Edwin Coddington. The Gettysburg Campaign (New York: Simon and Schuster, 1968): 7.
2. "General Index" The War of the Rebellion: A Compilation of the Official Records of the Union and Confederate Armies. John S. Moodey, Indexer. Washington:War Department, 1901. Preface, x. (Emphases added)

CHAPTER 4

Doubts Often Better Than Certainties

THE FIRST ACTUAL particle—minute, precious, and as cryptic as the absent planning records—came to light after the war. It's a bit of evidence washed down about the Northern campaign, one which careful readers of history can assay to determine its veridical purity, coming as it does from within the President's Cabinet. It demonstrates disturbing doubt about the leading general's 1863 plan to invade the North.

Neither Lee nor Davis ever publicly refuted that doubt, during the war or after, clearly indicating the doubt was hidden away in the war years. The particle is a diminutive trace: suspicion of Lee's fantastic plan. Something about the plan disturbed John H. Reagan.

The only member from the trans-Mississippi area of the Confederacy, Postmaster General Reagan was a Texas farmer and lawyer. Analytical, he was an independent thinker, still a bit woolly around the edges from his youthful years in the Smoky Mountains of east Tennessee. He remained in the Davis Cabinet throughout the war.

As a trusted friend, Reagan was the only member who stayed with Davis until they were captured in May 1865 by Union troops in Georgia—about ten miles from a place called Waterloo! Ironically, they were arrested in Irwin County, which had a powerful history of opposition to "Mr. Davis' war."

From its inception, the Confederacy had been fighting a two-front war: one against the North, another against disaffected and dissident Southerners … [O]ne editor had written in 1863 that Southerners were "fighting each other harder than we ever fought the enemy." … In the same month [June 1863] in Irwin County, local Unionists and a "large number of deserters" convened an anti-war meeting at Irwinville. They adopted several peace resolutions, including one calling for the Confederacy to surrender … In effect, Irwin County seceded from the Confederacy that day.[1]

From the start of the Confederate Secession onward, West Point-trained and Mexican War-baptized Jefferson Davis—later Secretary of War in President Franklin Pierce's administration—considered a *defensive* military strategy as the better Southern course of action to outlast Federal forces. He based his supposition on the North's preference for a short war as signified by President Abraham Lincoln's call for a *three*-month supply of volunteers. Lincoln didn't foresee a long war; a long-term army was not his plan to save the Union.

In May 1863 Jefferson Davis' leading general sought the exact opposite of his president's circumspect strategy. Lee wanted an *offensive* operation—into the underbelly of the foe! In the Confederate military planning meeting that month, Lee *versus* Davis became the issue.

The general was powerfully stimulated by his just-won glorious victory. At Chancellorsville he had whipped an army larger than his own. He thought another victory—of whatever kind—might end the conflict. Perhaps a unique "victory" at a unique time and a unique place could turn the tables for the Confederacy. The ever-increasing war machine of the North had to be sidetracked, nullified, taken out of the picture.

Added to that unusual appeal from Lee to have an offensive strategy match his offensive tactics, was the serious situation along the Mississippi River. Confederate leaders were compelled to consider that western theatre of war. Their Western army lay under vicious siege at Vicksburg by General "Unconditional Surrender" Grant. Their army needed reinforcements *post haste* and in huge numbers—from the east—that is, from Lee's Army of Northern Virginia. For Davis, a Mississippian, a decision clamped like an alligator at midnight in a cypress swamp, twisting and turning him cruelly. It added to his several physical illnesses. Notwithstanding, presidents must choose. The Mississippian living in Virginia had to choose: Mississippi or Virginia?

For Davis the selection was grim because his favorite commander didn't want to go westward but still wanted to move his Army of Northern Virginia. *Out* of Virginia. On the offense. *Elsewhere*: to a forgotten corner of American history.

Lee wanted to go "North to Pennsylvania!" Into a place without military significance or advantage, and for a strange reason. From a military perspective, "strange" is putting it mildly.

John Reagan opposed the plan. It didn't make sense.

Reagan probably had at least two reasons. First, the loss of Vicksburg would mean lost control of the Mississippi River, thereby cutting the Confederacy in two. The splitting of the Southern nation would be a separation of monumental proportions; geographically, politically, financially and militarily. John Reagan saw that Lee's plan gave moral support for Mississippi—yet not a single fighting unit for Vicksburg!

A second likely reason Reagan opposed the plan was that something about it smelled fishy—after three days dead fish reek to high heaven. It had an unknown quality that Lee apparently didn't make clear to the officials assembled in the President's office. His plan was but recently concocted, some seven days after the victory at Chancellorsville, and would not have been impressive militarily. It did not give the appearance of being fleshed out enough to tell Lee's whole story.

The first reason was self-evidently true. To anyone scrutinizing a global perspective of the war, lost control of the "Father of Waters" would be absolutely disastrous. Surveyed from Virginia to Texas, Florida to Missouri, Arkansas to North Carolina, crisscrossing the whole Confederacy, it was almost as evident as field cotton that the Mississippi Valley out west was the strategic heart of the South. Only a Southerner fixated on the eastern theatre of war could overlook the possible bad consequences of a plan to invade an area of the North devoid of military advantage. Lee was planning to march his army not to help protect the strategic heart of the Southland but to an unheralded place for a perplexing intention. It was not quite the Jaws of Death ... but why? *Where?*

The second reason Reagan opposed the plan is also sensible. As the President's inclination was for *defensive* strategy and the General's impulse was *offensive* action, an unsavory four-day stew of explanations, rationalizations, motives and pretexts, with stretches of truth and imagination, plus downright argumentativeness was cooked up 14-17 May 1863.

The officials present from time to time were the President, the General Commanding, the Secretary of War, the Adjutant General of the Confederate Army, and the Presidential Cabinet members. The meetings must have boiled over, for then they finally boiled down to the ill President acceding to Lee's unique plan. And the others swallowed the fare, finally. Or so it seemed, finally.

Davis had been suffering severely from a neurological facial affliction akin to "shingles," losing sight in one eye. And he was afflicted with the continuing effects of malaria. He also may have suffered his recurring stomach ailments, and possibly bronchitis, or an unfortunate admixture of several of those conditions. His Excellency was in bad shape. Physically, emotionally Jeff Davis was diminished we can say, without doubting our own truthfulness. That four-day stew must have seemed a Shakespearean witches' hell-broth, "wool of bat and tongue of dog/Adder's fork and blind-worm's sting," to no-nonsense lawyer John Reagan out of hardscrabble Texas.

The week after the decision, President Davis suffered harrowing pain again. The Cabinet met again to consider—actually, to re-consider—the Campaign. Without Lee.

Davis was reported to be "dangerously ill." Terribly weak, the President made the terribly wrong decision to support Lee. Commonly, terrible decisions beget terrible consequences.

After the Campaign's failure less than two years of warfare ravaged the South, savagery following savagery, terror upon terror. It wasn't John Reagan who caused it.

The situation was dismaying and the plan the leaders discussed in May 1863 was extravagant. John Reagan objected, writing later that Lee "believed he commanded an invincible army, which had been victorious in so many great battles, and all of them against greatly preponderating numbers and resources."[2] With remorse Reagan noted, "I could not expect, on such a question, to overrule the opinion of great military men like President Davis and General Lee."[3] So Lee's plan was adopted. Non-existent records can't tell the truth of how or why it was adopted—just as "dead men can't lie."

One wonders *if* or *how* those officials took Lee's romanticism and his personal distress over Jackson's demise into account. It could have been helpful for the President and others who attended the meetings to know that Robert Lee's two intellectual heroes were Hamlet and Don Quixote.[4] That a melancholic Dane who saw ghosts and a Spanish "knight" who "made the world laugh yet never cracked a joke" fed into Lee's conceptual and emotional processes is valuable information. But that process is not spectacular, therefore not given much credence, traditionally.

R. E. Lee's mental make-up surely must have crossed the mind of the one decision maker with whom Lee shared his West Point experience: Jefferson Davis. The former superb student cadet at West Point and later its Superintendent had to have been eloquent as he made an amazing intellectual case for his plan. Eloquence and prestige notwithstanding, John Reagan wrote later, "I will not now repeat the expressions I made when this conclusion was reached." Texas cowpuncher language didn't—and doesn't—sit well with "cultured" types, whether up North or down South. In the end, Postmaster Reagan noted, "We made a great mistake."[5]

A modern historian has written comprehensively about the Confederate Cabinet's final reconsideration of the Northern Campaign, a meeting behind closed doors that lasted "nearly all day" in late May 1863, before the army started moving northward. He has commented that the members reviewed the Northern Campaign, "though why that would have required a daylong discussion is hard to understand."[6]

Hard to understand? Hard to understand! Not if the historically golden nugget of John Reagan's reaction is considered as pointing to something unusual.

If Lee's plan had been about a battle to win a total and conclusive battle-to-end-all-battles in the war and to convincingly put a stop to simultaneous battles throughout the South, certainly John Reagan and other Confederate Cabinet members would have agreed pronto. Then the Cabinet would not have needed to gather in a totally impromptu fashion the very next day at the President's residence. Nor the next week in a formal session, for reevaluation of R. E. Lee's strange plan. Subsequently John Reagan would not have written in his memoir his fervid opposition to the peculiar plan.

Conversely to the modern historian, it *is* easy to understand why they had to have an extended discussion. It's possible to grasp the reason for the lengthy decision making, especially if the plan was inadequately formulated in multiple ways: militarily, politically, psychologically, or even spiritually.

When one amalgamates various precious particles of history that have come down to us including Reagan's opposition to R. E. Lee's plan of heading northward, what Lee intended to do, and where he was going, one discovers something unheard of in American military annals. "And that ain't just whistlin' 'Dixie,'" to quote another age's vernacular.

Chapter Notes
1. David Williams. Bitterly Divided: The South's Inner Civil War (N.Y.: New Press, 2008): 236-37.
2. John H. Reagan. Memoirs (N.Y.: Neale Publishing, 1906): 121-22.
3. Ibid.150-51.
4. Elizabeth Brown Pryor. Reading The Man (N.Y.: Viking, 2007): 464.
5. Reagan, Memoirs. 150 -51.
6. Steven E. Woodworth. Davis and Lee At War (Lawrence, KS: University Press of Kansas, 1995): 233.

CHAPTER 5

Familiarity Breeds ~~Contempt~~ Truth!

THE NEXT PRECIOUS particle washed down soon after the war's end. It was much like ear-to-wall eavesdropping because it came from the center of Confederate war strategy. The nugget informs us of an important fact about Robert Lee's Northern Campaign, and can change our understanding of it as well.

Its human source was close to the center of decision-making, but we're uncertain whether or not he was privy to actual planning sessions. His statements are not official in the sense of an authorized transcription of words from meetings. However, he was an official in spatial proximity to what was happening in the Confederate capital building. Competently placed in the government at Richmond, he was in-the-know, privy to confidential workings of the Confederacy at war.

Though a minor official, he was a published author who had been offered the position of *Chargé d'affaires*, representing the American government in Naples, Italy by John C. Calhoun, seventh Vice President of the United States when Secretary of State in the James Polk Administration. His appointment at the beginning of the Confederacy was recommended to President Jefferson Davis by former President of the United States John Tyler. This diarist was, by his admission in 1866, placed in a "very important position in the [Confederate] government until the end of its career."[1] He was like a personal secretary to the Secretary of War of the CSA, therefore rather knowledgeable of Southern intentions and actions.

Because records are missing, it isn't possible to determine whether or not he was in the President's office or close by at the time of any particular meetings. Nonetheless, as a source he is so authentic on different points of the war as to be quoted *extensively* in numerous proper historians' writings. Archivists down to our present time consider his two printed volumes of observations and notes reliable.

Sometimes the diarist's content cited mundane information about crop plantings and harvests, office comings and goings, weather reports, tittle-tattles and scuttlebutt about military promotions. Slightly more important subjects are included; he wrote about fears for Richmond's safety, anti-Jewish rants, dismay about one of his bosses, namely Secretary of War James H. Seddon, and about detested Northerners serving as officers in the Southern army—even though he had been a Northerner from New Jersey who went south after the bombardment of Fort Sumter.

Of somewhat more importance were his writings about his family garden, which provide evidence of the frightful food scarcity throughout the war, and ultimately, food riots in the South. He was deeply concerned that there were serious shortages of edible crops, but not of cotton and tobacco. The latter were big moneymakers during the war, while troops were often without food and people on the home front starved. Often he wrote of the raggedness of people's clothing, including his own; jealousies among administrative lackies were recorded *ad nauseum,* details which add minimal understanding of the somber issues of Secession and Rebellion.

Nonetheless, he frequently noted vital information concerning daily occurrences at Richmond, the War Department, arrivals and departures of military leaders and units, the health and ideas of President Davis, plus actions—and inactions—of Secretary of War Seddon, his immediate superior, concerning all things military and many things political. The diary is a literary Mulligan stew.

The minute and precious particles washing down from him are of far-reaching value, helping historians, later generations and buffs know what-was-what in Richmond from 1861 to 1865. John

Beauchamp Jones' 1866 publication, *A Rebel War Clerk's Diary At The Confederate States Capital*, gave day-by-day observations and notations of the war for four years. His Mulligan stew is tasty fare.

Two utterly important bits of information that Jones noted make quite possible the reshuffling of conventional views. The first such conventional view is that Lee planned a knock-out military battle against Federal forces to win the war on Northern soil; the second is that Lee planned to capture or destroy Harrisburg, Pennsylvania, a Northern state capital. Both views are hoary and uncomplicated for vested chroniclers, requiring no further analysis. The reasoning is that many "experts" have already accepted them, something like celebrities who by definition are famous-for-being-famous. Chroniclers with vested interests are advocates of what others with vested interests have already advocated. That way is easy. Whether it is accurate or not seems not to be a question for them.

Jones' diary entry for 16 May 1863, in the very week of the official planning sessions from 14 to 17 May in Richmond, broadcasted clearly—to those who would hear—the first of his two utterly important pieces of information. *"It appears, after the consultation of the generals and the President yesterday, it was resolved not to send Pickett's division to Mississippi … Gen. Lee is now stronger than before the battle* [of Chancellorsville] *… There is some purpose on the part of Gen. Lee to have a raid in the enemy's country,* **surpassing** *all other raids."* (Emphasis added)

Lo and behold! The Pennsylvania Campaign was not to be a general battle to defeat the North militarily as some people contended. It was to be a raid, a *surpassing raid*. It is said that "familiarity breeds contempt," but as philosopher Santayana wrote, "Familiarity breeds contempt only when it breeds inattention."[1] One would think paying attention to a published author serving in the Confederate War Department would breed truth.

What was the raid on that occasion intended to *surpass?* An army of 65,000-70,000 men to surpass the numbers in the opposing Union army? To do what? Spook Northerners? Satisfy Southerners? Occupy territory? Garrison farmland? Surpass Chancellorsville? Something serious is meant by the war clerk's use of "surpassing."

Obviously any raid would gather flocks, herds, and droves of animals and sundry supplies. Therein it succeeded. Lee's army raid into Pennsylvania farmland sent back to Virginia some 60,000 head of animals, lots of grain, and sundry other supplies, but primarily hardware. Horseshoes and more horseshoes for his beasts of burden and war stallions.

True, the raid gathered foodstuffs in amounts large enough to feed his army, thereby saving the livestock and supplies of Virginia farmers and growers. But was the number of animals seized to be the *surpassing* element of *all other raids*? Who would corral, feed, tend, and protect the multitudinous animals, if that's what it was about? Where would they store all the grains back in Virginia? Was Lee going to metamorphose his soldiers into herders and drovers, millers and draymen? Where would the animals be sheltered, pastured? In government stockyards? They didn't exist. Private barns? Allow the supplies to collect out in the open, exposed to the weather? Was Lee's plan to raid and secure one animal for each of his valiant warriors? If so, was he certifiably crazy to equate human life and animal life: 65,000-70,000 men for 60,000 livestock? What sense does it make to think the raid was a gigantic foraging expedition, exclusively for supplies *surpassing* all other raids? "That's mighty slim pickin's," Johnny Reb might well have said, "for an invincible army accustomed to winning battles."

Surely a forage raid as such would not have troubled Texas farmer John Reagan at the planning sessions. Everyone knew such a raid would have made sense because supplies were needed. But would a sensible raid make a hardheaded Texas lawyer oppose it enough to speak outrageously in the face of His Excellency Jefferson Davis? And jeopardize their close friendship? Or in the face of Robert Lee "whose fame now filled the world," as Reagan said of the Victor of Chancellorsville? Would Postmaster General Reagan have lost his cool like a petulant youth, before his professional colleagues in the

Cabinet?

But John Reagan did lose his cool. Some grave defect perceived in the plan raised the heat of the argument and lowered the civility of language. One can easily imagine the vitriol and crudeness of his language which years later he would not allow himself to repeat. Reagan was furious—to put it politely. The plan evoked antagonism and vitriol.

Undeniably, Reagan eventually acquiesced in what he called a "mistake." His regret ensued even before the failure of the Campaign. After the failure, Lee's mistaken plan dragged out total failure for almost two years of overflowing bloodletting.

Little known but highly respected by the Confederate president and his fellow cabinet members, John Reagan laid serious opposition in front of R. E. Lee's plan. His resistance robustly bespoke a bleak concern with the newspaper-designated "wisest, grandest, most imposing scheme" of R. E. Lee.

A precious particle shines forth indicating markedly that Lee was planning a Northern Campaign surpassing anything he had done before. A plan categorically different from anything he had done before, even when he had divided his army in the face of the enemy, a seemingly foolish, crippling maneuver. Is that what *surpassing* meant?

Chapter Notes

1. J. B. Jones. A Rebel War Clerk's Diary At The Confederate States Capital (Phila.: Lippincott, 1866): Vol. 1. iii.
2. George Santayana. The Sense of Beauty (Cambridge, MA: M.I.T. Press, 1988): 105.

CHAPTER 6

The Very Core

A REBEL WAR Clerk's Diary splashes down to us a second and utterly significant piece of information, a brilliant nugget of pure 24-carat historical gold. It tells in plain language what the Campaign was about. The telling of it in the understandable and startling words of a Confederate War Department secretary/clerk is what makes it so valuable.

The clerk was acquainted with the plan—to what degree is not known—more than was any other interpreter, historian, or devotee of Robert E. Lee's exploits. His attention to events and details made him a keen observer of the Confederate war effort. Previous to the war he had done the same as a recognized author of books on the American Far West.

This transformative archival gold gives specific information about Lee's wise, grand, imposing plan. Its writing overthrows the "received" interpretations of the purpose of the Pennsylvania Campaign. Along with the concept of a *surpassing* raid, this nugget incrementally clarifies—after a century and a half of guesswork—Lee's purpose for his Campaign. The diary entry announces:

June 30 [1863] *5 O'Clock P. M.*
The city [Richmond] *is now in good humor, but not wild with exultation. We have what seems pretty authentic intelligence of the taking of HARRISBURG the capital of Pennsylvania,*

> *the City of YORK, etc. etc. This comes on the flag of truce boat, and is derived from the enemy themselves. Lee will not descend to the retaliation instigated by petty malice; but proclaim to the inhabitants that all we desire is PEACE, not conquest.* (All emphases in original text)

General Robert E. Lee was planning to do something other than engage in a general battle. He was going to make a proclamation. His intent was to "proclaim ... PEACE." Most likely the intent was to offer an armistice. It was *not* to engage in war and conquest!

One has a right to be is puzzled, even flabbergasted, that this statement of Lee's intent has not been publicized. One can only wonder what purposes are served by neglect of that golden nugget when writing the story of the Northern Campaign, and its denouement: the Battle of Gettysburg.

The revelation gives an account contrary to the "received" views of Lee's intent in 1863, which exclusively construe his campaign as armed conflict. Are those interpreters of history correct and is war clerk John B. Jones a liar? How can it be that the observation of a person on the scene, where and when the Campaign was planned, is neglected or held to be of no account?

Jones asserted that the military commander would proclaim peace to the citizens of the North. One can assume that R. E. Lee would do so reasonably because he was a rational human being—most of the time. Reasonably, his plan probably included an armistice at the same time as Confederate Vice President Alexander Stephens was seeking an audience with his friend President Abraham Lincoln for a similar purpose, which also failed to occur. It would play to the burgeoning pro-South movements in the Northern states. Such movements for an end to the war had been active, expanding in numbers and import every day in Northern family houses. They expanded, as well, in newspapers. Even state political houses in the North expanded in end-the-war sentiment.

Lee's effort would be pacific while protected by the Army of Northern Virginia in its *surpassing* raid, looking conspicuously like an out-and-out military operation. The effort as planned would take his army to a special place he chose, not to a place of his adversary's choosing, and definitely not to the place speculated by his subordinate commanders in their euphoria after the recent magnificent victory at Chancellorsville.

That the war room clerk recorded emphatically just the day before the battle at Gettysburg what Lee would not do—and what he was about to do—demonstrates a significant point: General Lee's essence of strategy was deception. He remembered that a primary element in strategy is psychological warfare, to mystify the enemy as much as possible.

It was a secret, all a secret. Or so R. E. Lee thought.

But there was scuttlebutt. There's always scuttlebutt. This time the source was as close to General Lee as one could get, a personal aide. "Dawn of July 1 [1863] broke with a gentle breeze, and was sunshiny and clear, except for occasional showery clouds. ... [The commanding general] called to Longstreet to ride with him. The men of the First Corps were confident, and as they swung into the road, doubtless every one of them shared the view Lee's adjutant general had expressed in a letter two days before: 'With God's help we expect to take a step or two toward an honorable peace.'"[1]

Adjutant General Walter H. Taylor knew something very important about General Lee's plans: an *honorable* peace. In a step or two. After a proclamation of peace—and no "general battle"—followed by negotiations.

A proclamation of peaceful intentions by an invading general, not victory or conquest, certainly qualifies as mystification of the highest order: a plan *nonpareil*.

And a minute particle of historical gold from the Robert E. Lee's scribe is matchless as well.

Chapter Note

1. Douglas Southall Freman. R. E. Lee: A Biography (N.Y.: Scribner's, 1934): Vol. III. 65.

CHAPTER 7

Attempted Strategy

IT WAS JUNE 1863 and Robert Lee was disappointed with some of his soldiers. Depredation of Maryland by some Army of Northern Virginia soldiers during his first incursion across the Potomac River in September '62 had disturbed his sensitivities about how a Christian soldier acts.[1] Therefore, to accomplish his noble effort for peace he instituted an order, which *"will be strictly observed,"* not to molest Northerners nor their property.

GENERAL ORDERS, HDQRS. ARMY OF NORTHERN VIRGINIA
NO. 73   *Chambersburg, PA., June 27, 1863*

The commanding general has observed with marked satisfaction the conduct of the troops on the march, and confidently anticipates results commensurate with the high spirit they have manifested.

No troops could have displayed greater fortitude or better performed the arduous marches of the past ten days.

Their conduct in other respects has, with few exceptions, been in keeping with their character as soldiers and entitles them to approbation and praise.

There have, however, been instances of forgetfulness, on the part of some, that they have in keeping the yet unsullied reputation of the army, and that the duties exacted of us by civilization and Christianity are not less obligatory in the country of the enemy than in our own.

The commanding general considers that no greater disgrace could befall the army, and through it our whole people, than the perpetration of the barbarous outrages upon the unarmed and defenseless and the wanton destruction of private property, that have marked the course of the enemy in our own country.

Such proceedings not only degrade the perpetrators and all connected with them, but are subversive of the discipline and efficiency of the army, and destructive of the ends of our present movement.

It must be remembered that we make war only upon armed men, and that we cannot take vengeance for the wrongs our people have suffered without lowering ourselves in the eyes of all whose abhorrence has been excited by the atrocities of our enemies, and offending against Him to Whom vengeance belongeth, without Whose favor and support our efforts must all prove in vain.

The commanding general therefore earnestly exhorts the troops to abstain with most scrupulous care from unnecessary or wanton injury to private property, and he enjoins upon all officers to arrest and bring to summary punishment all who shall in any way offend against the orders on this subject.

R. E. LEE *General*

There isn't a real question whether or not General Lee intended a peaceful invasion, a calm, undisruptive intrusion preceding a proclamation of peace. He didn't want trouble with Northern civilians.

Astutely rational and just as a leader of men, Lee gave evidence he knew an important truth: The *means* a person uses to accomplish a goal commonly earn as much merit as does actually reaching the *ends* desired.

The equivalence of *means* and *ends* gives further evidence Robert Lee understood the new study, psychology. That subject was first viewed as "psychological character" by Isaac D'Israeli, the father of English Prime Minister Benjamin Disraeli, in his widely read 1812 study *Calamities and Quarrels of Authors*. Lee practiced a hands-on psychology in the midst of warfare to gain peace by any "honorable means."[2]

Such an undertaking was phenomenal wartime policy, but understandable if peace and independence were the goals—and before attrition, decay, and opposition set in because of the atrocities, brutalities, and casualties. And R. E. Lee was the man for the task. Audacious in war, he was ardent for peace. In 1863 he was especially keen, fired up for peace. His Campaign was not a raid to conquer, to punish, to defeat an enemy, *unless attacked*. He had a wise design, a grand concept to gain peace, an imposing strategy to match the best efforts of the best military leaders who ever did battle.

The precious particle about his *raid surpassing all other raids* would not have been a military action as such, but could have become one if attacked. Lee assumed something unfortunate: Northern officials would somehow realize that his 65,000-70,000 fighting men were not going to do battle! He gave no inkling that they were short-term raiders gathering livestock and supplies and were simply escorting him to do something unknown! He must have assumed that as he moved northward from Chancellorsville they would consider his movements non-threatening and a wasteful effort. Lee was confident the Federals would proceed cautiously, move in a direction generally away from his army in order to protect Washington, D.C. just in case he might use trickery to catch them off guard. Or that his northward movement would uncover Richmond, enticing the Northern army to head toward the Southern Capital to capture it.

Of course Lee, ever secretive, never hinted to Northern sources that he was not intending to fight a general battle. Psychological warfare can psych out its practitioners, too.

Nor did he tell or hint of his plan to his own people—*especially* his own officers and men. Lee's conviction that secrecy is the core of military deception precluded him from telling the story—and the whole story, particularly—to anyone from President Davis down through the political chain of command to his own officers and men. No one else dared know, and therefore they could not know.

In addition to thinking that the Northern army would stay back to protect Washington, Lee seems to have thought that any Yankees who might be in the area would realize that his army was not conducting itself as a conquering horde—particularly when it didn't have to face any military opposition upon entering Maryland and then Pennsylvania. Unmistakably, his army was not damaging homes or bombarding villages and towns. The countryside was not visibly vandalized in the areas the Army of Northern Virginia traversed. The troops were not engaging in combative acts and certainly were not scorching the earth in vengeance for Northern invasion of Southern lands.

He must have supposed his army's non-aggressive actions would be obvious to Northern officials, military and political. They didn't have a great sense of place, as Southerners had of Dixieland, therefore the Yankees wouldn't act possessively and take a chance at a disastrous third defeat. Lee had to have assumed that because his army's actions were not belligerent and violent, that any Yankee forces in the area would not obstruct his rather *irenic* movement into southcentral Pennsylvania, where nothing of military value existed. The Northern Army of the Potomac would avoid his army, fearful of a third-in-a-row defeat after his great victories at Fredericksburg and Chancellorsville

Lee's overly emphasized secrecy meant he shielded information from Northerners about anything—anything at all. It was a strange mindset, as secrecy always is. Robert Edward Lee forgot that strange ideas beget strange results.

Like liars, who must have a good memory for facts or they'll be caught in their lying, secret bearers also require a good memory. They also must consider what will happen when others perceive their secret to be something quite different from what the secret bearer knows it is. In plain words, just as a rose is a rose is a rose, so R. E. Lee's secret turned out to be an invasion is an invasion is an invasion, to Northerners. Their soil was precious, too.

To his credit—if credit it be—General Lee would have his army prepared and alert should the enemy treat his invasion as an invasion and then attack first.

That readiness and willingness to fight clouded his rationality. Secretly! Sundry times, deception deceives deceivers.

Lee's upheld strategy of deception in warfare failed him in his Pennsylvania Campaign. He inflated deception and it collapsed on him. His actions looked *exclusively military*; one would search a long time to find someone who thought it to be otherwise.

He framed his effort wrongly; no one could see it as peaceful. Even though the purpose of the *surpassing raid* was peace-seeking, it could be seen only as confrontational. It didn't even look peaceable to the Southern army in the North.

He spelled out his reason for the Northern Campaign in his official report to Confederate officials, shortly after the failure at Gettysburg, so people could know something about his intent:

> "It <u>had not been intended to fight a general battle</u> at such a distance from our base, <u>unless attacked</u> by the enemy, but finding ourselves unexpectedly confronted by the Federal Army, it became a matter of difficulty to withdraw through the mountains with our large trains [of supply] a battle thus became, in a measure, unavoidable."[1]

And Confederate President Davis had concurred emphatically, adding an insight:

"It <u>had not been intended to deliver a general battle</u> at such a distance as Gettysburg from our base [in Virginia] *<u>unless attacked</u>; ... If* [success] *could be done <u>by maneuvering merely,</u> a most important result would be cheaply attained."*[2]

One either accepts that Lee and Davis were honorable or were liars. Were they seeking a general battle or not—that is, a full-blown Chancellorsville-type knock-down, drag 'em out battle to end the whole war? Did Lee lie in his report during the war to cover a multitude of errors and did Davis prevaricate after the war, in his book, to justify the Southern cause?

The first position, Lee and Davis as honorable men who did not intend a general battle, is *possible*, although *militarily unsound*. Had Lee won an overarching victory in Pennsylvania, Federal armies still would have operated elsewhere in the Confederacy and would have carried on their battles regardless of what happened in a small corner of the Union.

The second position is *weird* and *beyond belief.* The second— that both men were liars—stems from a "mind already made up," a prejudgment. It is a prejudice that unfairly condemns two decent men who are monumental in American history. True, both men were misguided and misguiding, yet neither was ever tried by a jury nor found guilty of anything, certainly not of lying.

One can dance around their recorded statements or one can accept the dance itself, joining a real Virginia Reel with Lee and Davis. Lee's plan may have been quixotic, extravagant and risky, but his purpose was peace. All for peace, by any honorable means.

Robert Edward Lee imagined the South would become independent only by using reason in negotiation. Destruction in victorious battles against armies larger and stronger had provided exceeding little gain for Confederates in two years of warfare. Southerners needed to realize that just as dedicated Union forces had failed, dedicated Rebels would fail sooner or later. They didn't realize it would be sooner.

If war continued, the North still would proceed building the transcontinental railroad system; it would still settle and farm the verdant Plain States; its industries would open more gold and silver mines; its northeastern population would increase wagon trains full of pioneers migrating to populate the Far West. It had done so since the war began in 1861 and it would continue. As the North would increase its geographic area, it would bear greater influence in the world community. The North was a lively work-in-progress.

On the other hand the South, defeated *or* victorious, would be left with a hankering for what the North had and for what it had done. But envy doesn't build anything: not roads or confidence; not cross-country railroads or employee-sustaining businesses; not farms that produce food for families rather than tobacco smokes for addicts or cotton for boll weevils. Southerners would have to try to duplicate Northern success—with slave labor growing tobacco and cotton until its depleted soil would collapse. Its people would cry out for relief and release as the political South would stand immobilized, on the outside of a world cranking up industries and modernizing with new inventions. The pre-war culture of class separations and privileges wouldn't be able to compete.

The South would have to seek deliverance, deliverance from its failed ideas of both human slavery and absolutist state sovereignty. It had violated the principle of Perpetual Union from Benjamin Franklin to the Founders of the Republic, in both the constitutions they promulgated: the Articles of Confederation and Perpetual Union of 1777 and its improvement in the Constitution of 1787 *"in Order to form a more perfect Union."*

Had its two leaders, Lee and Davis, lied purposely in their reports—as is implied in the assertion that the invasion was for the purpose of triumphing in one massive general battle to win the war—their crime, or sin, would have compromised the very integrity of the Southern cause. Their fabrication would have impugned their integrity to their graves.

Such lying would have been tantamount to vilifying the

honored Southern dead and mocking all the men still serving after the Pennsylvania Campaign. Likewise, it would have repudiated the South's principled opposition to a centralized government in Washington, D.C. Without a question in the world, if Lee and Davis had lied about not seeking a general battle, unless attacked, they would have defiled every last Confederate soldier who had been slain or wounded. The sacrifices and sufferings of tens of thousands of Southern lives and families would not only have been trivialized but mocked, as well. If Lee and Davis had lied it would have hopelessly impoverished and wrecked Southern society, yes, even Southern character.

The words of those highest Confederate leaders were their bonds, lifelong. It follows that the statement "no general battle, unless attacked" meant *"no ... general battle ... unless ... attacked."* One is bewildered that those statements could be misunderstood, overlooked, denied—except by people with vested interests.

No matter who or how many contend that Davis and Lee planned a war-ending battle, they've missed the man Robert Edward Lee and put an end to his very character. And they've cheated Jefferson Finis Davis by making him a twenty-first century Washington politician.

J. B. Jones, in the War Department of the Confederacy, and his precious particle glisten: The purpose of the Northern Campaign was to *"proclaim to the inhabitants that all we desire is PEACE, not conquest."*

R. E. Lee hadn't wanted to feel the same way in his Northern Campaign of 1863 as he had felt in the invasion of September '62— disappointed and defeated. The troops who had depredated and damaged Maryland in that earlier invasion had damaged him also. He didn't deserve such treatment. Nor did Maryland deserve what those Southern "gentlemen" had done.

After the Fourth of July 1863, disappointment and defeat doubled in Dixie.

Chapter Notes

1. The War Of The Rebellion: A Compilation Of The Official Records Of The Union And Confederate Armies. Washington: War Department, 1889. Series 1. 27. 308. 31 July 1863. (Hereafter referred to as WR:OR) (Emphases added)

2. Jefferson Davis. The Rise and Fall of the Confederate Government (N.Y.: Appleton, 1881): Vol. 2. 442-443. (Emphasis added)

CHAPTER 8

Unknown "New" Man

VARIOUS FLECKS OF historical gold have come down to us from R. E. Lee himself, explaining himself, yet many don't want to accept or even acknowledge this "new" man.

Lee is different from people's invested idea of who and what is the real R. E. Lee. For example, he did not sign his name Robert E. Lee the way we like to see and hear it; he *always* signed his name R. E. Lee, even when writing to his wife and children. R. E. Lee, without fail, used the truncated form.

A *non-military* Robert E. Lee is too much for people to accept, especially those who only acknowledge what they've been told about him and who don't assent to what he became.

As a youth R. E. Lee studied under a Quaker schoolmaster, Benjamin Hallowell. He learned languages, sciences, and was drilled in mathematics. How much more or what else he learned from the Quaker we don't know. To suppose he didn't encounter and learn values integral to the Society of Friends is to suppose inadequately.

The young Lee had wanted to attend Harvard, as his brother Charles had. Harvard would requite his intellectual love: mathematics. His mother Ann hadn't wanted him to attend the United States Military Academy, but as an abandoned wife become a widow, she couldn't afford a Harvard education for the lad.

Still, becoming an army officer might help restore the family's honor, destroyed by his military father's unlucky financial dealings, romantic dalliances, his subsequent slip-away to the Caribbean area and pathetic shenanigans there. Henry "Light-Horse Harry" Lee was the center of gossip in the balmy Caribbean. In his abandoned Virginia stamping ground Henry Lee was the talk of the town. Of course, the dumped family at 607 Orinoco Street, Alexandria, heard only whispers amidst their sobs and sighs.

On their parts, wife, mother and children talked little with others about "Light-Horse" running away. However, they did talk about husband and father: in prayers. They appealed to God for his return, and gave thanks for the wide family of mother Ann Hill Carter Lee who assisted them over the years in various circumstances.

The fame of General Henry "Light-Horse Harry" Lee of the Revolutionary War had passed into oblivion. He had spawned legal problems after that war, mainly financial troubles due to land speculation that resulted in economic ruin for him—and others.

Such a problem was not all that unusual for the times. "This was an era in which chronic debtors weren't just bumblers but criminals."[1] A few years earlier *the* legal scholar of the 1787 Constitutional Convention, James Wilson, had been in terrible financial circumstances. He had been Benjamin Franklin's spokesman in the Convention as well as co-authority with James Madison on ancient and contemporaneous political systems. It was Wilson who put forth in the Constitution of 1787 the workable—but odious—compromise on slavery: a slave is to be counted as three-fifths a person. During Washington's presidency Wilson had speculated so wildly on land he was sent to debtor's prison—though at the time he was a sitting Associate Justice of the United States Supreme Court appointed by President Washington! In prison he read novels, not history, not law. Henry Lee's speculations were of the same kind as Justice Wilson's, except he imprisoned himself in the Caribbean. He didn't read novels: his companion was rum.

"Light-Horse Harry" had been a personal friend of George Washington. It was he who had pronounced the famous tribute of Congress to President Washington: "First in war, first in peace, first in the hearts of his countrymen." However, Henry "Light-Horse Harry" Lee, brave cavalry commander in war, ran away from his own conflict to the Caribbean, never again to see his family. Self-tortured, alone.

The boy Bobbie was six years old when his father deserted the family. Lacking a father figure, he was a miniature adult caring for his mother, a boy abandoned in a man's world. Terrible things go on in a child's mind when a parent runs away: Did I do something wrong? Love cries out: Did I drive him away? Abandonment is imprisonment for a child. Father Henry died in 1818 when the lad was 11 years old.

With hope destroyed of a father to lead him, the young man Robert was, as it were, in solitary confinement. If, however, he became military, his family's good name might be restored. Possibly his father's reputation could be mended, rehabilitated. R. E. Lee became a military man.

When he was graduated from West Point in 1829 his mother's trust was fulfilled. Ann Hill Carter Lee died the very next month, her work completed. At age twenty-two R. E. Lee was without parents to help correct a twisted boyhood and a stressed adolescence into a straight and tall Cedar of Lebanon. He had to plant, water, and nurture himself into adulthood.

With emotional duress enduring from childhood, through military assignments, to war, to political division, to another war, to defeat, it is no wonder the former general said after the war, "The great mistake of my life was taking a military education."[2] Also on his lips was, "The greatest mistake I ever made was becoming a soldier."[3] In a letter to his former Corps commander, Richard Ewell, Lee averred, "For my part I much enjoy the charms of civil[ian] life. I find too late I have *wasted* the best years of my existence."[4] The great general acknowledged that his prior life was a great error.

It's understandable, then, that sometime in the last five years of his life while he was President of Washington College in Lexington, Virginia, Lee stopped researching material related to his own life. His research concerned military matters preparatory to writing a book, but not about himself.

Lee's purpose was worthy: He wanted to write in order to extol his men in the ranks, giving credit to them. To them, not to himself. Not to their officers, either. The book was to be about the footsloggers, the nondescript, the shoeless, the undecorated, the unknown, the hungry, those who fought for something more than slavery—to the brave, the brave, and thrice brave.

Even with its noble purpose, Robert Lee stopped the literary effort. He was a different man: his own man. His own man as a post-war educator, not a warrior. He was making a difference by preparing young men for service to others, to Virginia, to the South, to the nation. As a leader, the son of General "Light-Horse" Harry helped the young men of Washington College to live and to help others to live. As educator he was not making young men into warriors to kill others. Lee the college president was a different man from the officer who had resigned his military commission in the army of the United States of America to follow Virginia into the Confederate States of America and into war against the army of the United States of America.

Many people do not accept Lee's own words rejecting his past. "Lee couldn't have said *that!*" is an exclamation of the uninformed. Truth is, Lee was and is more than the general that one-dimensional followers and writers have portrayed him to be. The words he spoke about himself when he matured into full humanness after the war are no less R. E. Lee than the orders he gave during the war. In fact, those words crown his life.

Robert Edward Lee's fame cloaks the power of his tongue and the truth of his heart. Fame fades, however: after the best is told, fame is but a name—signifying little.

Character holds firm. After all is said, character changes lives. It changes lives that change other lives—through the years, throughout centuries.

Many miss that glorious treasure of Lee's character, a character that holds firm.

Chapter Notes

1. Dennis Drabelle. "Flawed Founder," The Pennsylvania Gazette. (University of Pennsylvania) May-June 2011, 51. See Pp. 46-51.

2. C. B. Flood. Lee: The Last Years (Boston: Houghton Mifflin, 1981): 15.

3. M. Fishwick. Lee After The War (Westport, Ct.: Greenwood Press, 1963): 74.

4. J. W. Jones. Personal Reminiscences,Ancedotes ,and Letters of Robert E. Lee (N.Y.: Aberknopf, 1875): 117-18. (Emphasis added)

CHAPTER 9

"They Shall Be Called the Children of God"

SO PERSUADED ARE most Americans of Lee's military prowess, they've not seen his virtue as a peaceable human being.

It is true that R. E. Lee duty-bound himself to Virginia and that commitment resulted in his becoming a general. As a result people lock themselves into thinking of him exclusively in military terms. It is easy to do so because it always has been easy to do so.

Yet, a year before the Pennsylvania Campaign, he sent a message to the Confederate President requesting a *peace* proposal be sent to the North. It is another nugget of truth shunted down to us, a precious particle shining brightly to those who want to know what Lee was.

> September 8, 1862.
> His EXCELLENCY JEFFERSON DAVIS,
> President of the Confederate States, Richmond, Va.:
>
> MR. PRESIDENT,
>
> The present position of affairs, in my opinion, places it in the power of the government of the Confederate States to propose with propriety that of the United States to the recognition of our independence. For more than a year both sections of the country have been devastated by hostilities which have

brought sorrow and suffering upon thousands of homes, without advancing the objects which our enemies proposed to themselves in beginning the contest. Such a proposition, coming from us at this time, could in no way be regarded as suing for peace; but, being made when it is in our power to inflict injury upon our adversary, would show conclusively to the world that our sole object is the establishment of our independence and the attainment of an honorable peace. The rejection of this offer would prove to the country that the responsibility of the continuance of the war does not rest upon us, but that the party in power in the United States elect[s] to prosecute it for purposes of their own. The *proposal of peace* would enable the people of the United States to determine at their coming elections whether they will support those who favor a prolongation of the war, or those who wish to bring it to a termination, which can but be productive of good to both parties without affecting the honor of either. (Emphasis added)

I have the honor to be, with great respect,
Your obedient servant,
R. E. Lee, *Gen.*

Unquestionably Lee could have voiced the words of a philosopher, "The soldier, above all other people, prays for peace, for he must suffer and bear the deepest wounds and scars of war ... 'Only *the dead have seen the end of war,'*"[1] words later quoted at West Point by General Douglas MacArthur in 1962. Lee even anticipated MacArthur's hallowed words, "*Duty. Honor. Country.*" He happily could have vocalized the resonant tones of MacArthur spoken a hundred years after his own desire for peace was expressed formally in that 1862 proposal to President Davis to seek peace.

Peace had been the thread though the necklace of freedom for Lee. He would give all beads—Northern and Southern—their particular appeal, special place, and enduring value, *if* rational people would meet to restore themselves to the beauty, to the worth, to the blessings of freedom *for each another.*

One of R. E. Lee's personal habits was to garner information of the human world around him always. No one, therefore, has ever questioned the fact that he read Northern newspapers, whenever he could get them, for general information about the North, as well as news of the North's military movements. Assuredly, then, he would have been cognizant of the Great Peace Convention planned for 3 June 1863 in New York City, before he laid his plans in mid-May. The Northern peace movement had coalesced months before, in February 1863, three months before his victory at Chancellorsville and five months before his loss at Gettysburg.

> In the fall 1862 elections, after the preliminary [Emancipation] Proclamation, Peace Democrats [made] a bid for power. In [N.Y.] city ex-mayor Wood and his supporters denounced the [Lincoln] administration as "fanatical, imbecile, and corrupt" and openly urged resistance. … The peace movement continued to build after the full Proclamation was issued [1 January 1863]. On February 6, 1863 a group of Democratic and ex-nativist businessmen launched the Society for the Diffusion of Political Knowledge. Other luminaries included venerable Samuel F. B. Morse, president, and [N.Y.] Governor Seymour, … the organization published anti-war and anti-emancipation tracts … and agitated for a negotiated peace and the revocation of emancipation … [and] also promoted these ideas in the *New York World.*[2]

Lee, then, would have known of such developments. They would have entered his decision-making processes and come to a head after his victory at Chancellorsville.

The peace convention was peopled with Northerners who thought the war was unjust: the South was being treated wrongly … and meanly. Held at the Cooper Institute in New York City, various peace groups, not only Abolitionists, were in attendance. The meeting had been well publicized for weeks by Benjamin Wood, editor of the *New York Daily News*. Wood's brother, the so-called "cunning scoundrel" Fernando Wood, when he had been His Honor the Mayor of New York, had wanted to proclaim the largest city in America a free city. In that posture, New York was to be neither Northern nor Southern. It amounted to a semi-detachment from the Union—tantamount to another secession. Lincoln and the rest of the North could not have that rupture.

A pot of near-insurrection was brewing up North that Abraham Lincoln could not chill down easily; using force would cause it to boil fiercely. His main army had suffered two major military defeats. His presidency was sinking in status prior to the coming election. Lincoln was stymied. Lee's army was inching northward.

It was a propitious time for the Army of Northern Virginia to be marching northward. The Confederate Commander, avid newspaper reader, had to have known about the well-published peace movement. It would become part of his plan. Capitalizing on the bitter war opposition occurring across the North, Robert Edward Lee was no man's fool; timing would be a huge factor in his unique campaign *"to proclaim peace ... not conquest."* The Great Peace Convention was so significant that Lee's Major General Dorsey Pender wrote to his wife Fanny on 9 June 1863, "public sentiment in the North must and will do us good."

Nor can anyone seriously question that Lee knew of another upcoming effort for peace. This one was involved the Vice President of the Confederacy, Alexander H. Stephens. The VP urged President Davis to open negotiations with the Union government regarding the exchange of military prisoners.

Stephens had written a 12 June 1863 letter to Jefferson Davis about three weeks before Lee was at Gettysburg:

> I think I might do some good—not only on the *immediate* subject in hand [prisoner exchange] but in conference with

the authorities at Washington on *any* point in relation to the *conduct* of the war, I am not without hopes, that *indirectly*, I could now turn attention to a *general* adjustment, upon such a basis as might ultimately be acceptable to both parties. (All emphases in original)

Stephens was confident that his decades-long friendship with Abraham Lincoln, dating back to their service together in the U. S. House of Representatives, would help him discuss with Northern authorities "*any* point," and even "turn attention to a *general* adjustment" about ending the war.

Lee was in the loop as indicated by the Rebel war clerk: "We *all* knew about the mission of Vice-President Stephens under [a] flag of truce. It was ill-timed for success."[3]

In other words, peace was in the air, South and North. The carnage of war distressed nearly every person, Blue or Gray, its stench in the air day-by-day for Americans on both sides of the Mason-Dixon Line, as each the other blamed.

Lee chose to breathe the air of peace, not the stifling air of a public forum nor the hot air of a one-man show. He breathed the air of his Christian faith: "Blessed are the peacemakers: for they shall be called the children of God."[4]

The Commanding General of the Army of Northern Virginia had something of that faith in mind two years into the war. Two years were long enough for a civil war—a war doing no one any good. He had a peace intention of his own two years before his Northern Campaign and resultant battle at Gettysburg. It was a different kind of calculation for peace.

Wise and grand and imposing, the plan still was hazardous, even quixotic. In the form of a wartime invasion, Lee's plan did not call for hot musket lead or fiery cannonballs of conquest. It did call for no-nonsense words proclaiming peace to Northern inhabitants to start again the American experience.

It was a gamble. Peace always is as much a gamble as war; one never knows how such towering human efforts can go awry so easily.

And initiating a peace venture is a mighty gamble: The first to move boldly is in the open, can easily be shot down. But the mightiest gamble is that the chance for peace can be missed altogether.

It was shameful that R. E. Lee's peaceful pursuits were missed—and still are.

Chapter Notes

1. George Santayana. Soliloquies In England (N.Y.: Scribner's, 1922): 102. (Written after World War I)
2. P. Burrows & M. Wallace. Gotham: a history of New York City to 1898. N.Y.: Oxford University Press, 1998. 560.
3. Jones, Rebel War Clerk's Diary. I. 377. (Emphasis added)
4. Holy Bible (AV). Matt. 5: 9.

CHAPTER 10

Secrecy Again ... Even When It Hurts

ROBERT EDWARD LEE was a peace-seeker—but kept that fact secret from his sub-commanders—as was his wont. "Lee's penchant for secrecy excluded [even] his chief officers, who understandably failed to coordinate on a battle plan about which they knew nothing."[1]

His secrecy is a nugget that has come down to us, though it is not a shining example of the man. High-level secrecy was necessary for a leader who had the lives of thousands of human beings in his hands. But high-level secrecy harms something exceedingly important: communication.

A secret is a muscular force in human communication. In wartime it is much more potent. Wartime secrecy is far more robust and mighty when there are inklings, intimations, or hints about it on any side of an issue. Half a truth is better than none, *and* half a lie works more magic than an outright lie because it resembles a true statement.

As well, a secret—full lie or half-truth—has the air of the unfamiliar, of intrigue, about it. When accompanied by a tinge of the unlikely, the bizarre element in secrecy builds castles in the air, or dungeons underground. A secret often has a power that intimates it can overwhelm everything in its path.

Therefore, a secret cannot fail to excite interest, stirring, as it does, the pot of suspicion with the ladle of exaggeration over a fire of anxiety. In other words, a secret focuses attention, sometimes more than does explicit declaration. The upshot of such centered attention can heighten enthusiasm for a cause, or strike alarm in an opponent. It is no wonder that secrecy is an integral part of the *armamentarium* of a general about to do a great deed.

It must be said—although much about Lee's secrecy is unknown and thus can't be said—that secrecy was not simply part of his ordinary social reserve nor was it something arcane or melodramatic. His use of secrecy was pragmatic and necessary. Its use was not like gossiping for ego satisfaction nor was it a trivialization of others—even of enemies for self-promotion. Yet when his secrecy was un-actualized, that is, when it didn't accomplish its intended purpose, people involved were left feeling distant and insecure, frighteningly close to being bewildered.

Lieutenant Colonel G. W. Lay, a member of Lieutenant General P. G. T. Beauregard's staff said, "neither he [Beauregard] *nor anyone* is capable of sounding the profound plans of Lee."[2] Excluded from his secret plans, R. E. Lee's men were unable to fathom the nature or intricacies of his intent in heading northward after his failed attempt to do something similar, less than a year before, had ended in defeat at Sharpsburg/Antietam, Maryland. The ground they traveled over was familiar, the purpose obscure.

As such, Lee's secrecy left much to be desired because it was complete quietude, wordlessness.

In Lee's Northern Campaign his plan was unrealized because it was *unrealizable*. The secrecy finally became damaging to the Confederate cause, certainly in the Eastern Theater of operations, but overall as it lugged ominous recollections from Gettysburg with it. In that sense it was rather like fool's gold, i.e., pyrite, iron sulfide, FeS_2. Fool's gold glistens and is beautiful in its own way due to similarity in color, form, and habitat with gold—but it is not the real stuff, *Au*, gold. The Northern Campaign had negative worth for Lee's fighting men; they had no bragging rights, no dramatic clashes won, no victorious highpoints. Valor yes, mastery no. Dedication yes, supremacy no. Gettysburg wiped out both Chancellorsville and Fredericksburg as significant victories; wiped them off the scoreboard of the war.

Secrecy costs. John B. Jones, the Rebel war clerk, in his diary entry of 26 June 1862 stated categorically, "It is characteristic of Lee's secretiveness to keep *all* of his officers in profound ignorance of his intentions ..." (Emphasis in original)

As well, Jones variously wrote of Lee's long periods of silence about his campaigns. "We get nothing from Lee himself."[3] Not even a familial relationship broke what seems like a code of silence: "Colonel Custis Lee, from the President's office, was in my office ... and said nothing had been received from his father."[4] Silence brought negativity with it: "The absence of dispatches from Gen. Lee himself is beginning to create distrust"[5] and, "The Secretary of War has caught the prevailing alarm at the silence of Lee, and posted off to the President [Davis] for a solution—but got none."[6]

Sharply to the point, some of Lee's own division commanders told the same alarming story of the Commanding General's outright preference for secrecy. Major General George E. Pickett, the hero of the bizarre "Pig War" with Great Britain that happened in the Pacific Northwest two years before civil war broke out in the eastern states, knew the value of clear orders. At the San Juan Islands, where the Puget Sound meets the Strait of Juan de Fuca, Pickett earned his military spurs amidst changing orders and subtle movements of opponents. With that experience in mind he wrote a critique to his future wife, Sallie Ann Corbell, about R. E. Lee's *modus operandi*. In a letter dated 27 June 1863, four days before the battle at Gettysburg, General Pickett noted, "The object of this [present] great march is, of course, *unknown* to us. Its purpose and destination are known at present only to the Commanding General and his Chief Lieutenants." What those three corps commanders knew—if they knew anything at all—is anyone's guess.

Another division commander, William Dorsey Pender, the rising star among Lee's generals, wrote several times to his wife of Lee's secrecy. Pender was twenty-nine years old when Lee recommended him for promotion to Major General after his valor in the Chancellorsvile Confederate victory, observing, "Pender is an excellent officer, attentive, industrious, and brave: [he] has been conspicuous in every battle, and I believe wounded in almost all of them."

In the bargain Pender was a truth-teller, ardently seeking personal salvation, important to him because it was of supreme importance to his wife, Fanny, who feared greatly for her husband's immortal soul. The secrecy became heart-rending to them when Pender realized he was marching into Northern territory with Lee. It turned piteous when she contended Lee's action was contrary to the Will of God. Fanny Pender contended that by becoming invaders rather than virtuous defenders of their homeland, the South would see God withdraw His blessings from the Southern cause. The situation grew wretched when the pregnant twenty-three-year-old became a widow, suffering the loss of her husband, Dorsey, who had been wounded at Gettysburg and died shortly thereafter.

Corps commander, Lt. General A. P. Hill, wrote of Pender, "No man fell during the bloody battle of Gettysburg more regretted than he, nor around whose youthful brow were clustered brighter rays of glory."[7] Commanding General Lee wrote, "The loss of Major-General Pender is severely felt by the army and the country. He served with this army from the beginning of the war, and took a distinguished part in all its engagements ... His promise and usefulness as an officer were only equaled by the purity and excellence of his private life."[8]

General Pender was notable. What he observed about Lee's secrecy is notable, too: "We have rumors as to the future but know nothing in reality. If keeping [one's] own counsel goes to constitute a general, Lee possesses that to perfection."[9] And General Pender died serving Lee's silence.

Silence, taken to perfection, still would be a foible, a quirk, an idiosyncratic limitation. If silence could be made perfect, it is good to remember that extremes in virtues become injurious, as do vices, generally.

A shorter time before the bloodiest battle of the war, at Gettysburg, Pender had written, "Thus far Gen. Lee's plans have worked admirably says Gen. Hill [Pender's immediately superior officer] *who I suppose knows them. I do not ...*"[10]

Suppose? A general-rank officer *supposing* his immediate superior knows a master plan! If Hill knew, he never told Pender or any other of his division commanders, as far as we know. Lee evidently did not inform any of his division commanders who were leading their men—somewhere. But where? Secrecy in his Northern Campaign soon became vacuous. Deadly, too.

That last letter that Pender ever wrote was penned three days before the spectacular—but still unexpected—battle of Gettysburg, and sums up the paucity of information with which the Army of Northern Virginia lived. Other than their heading northward, the army did not know where Lee was leading them or exactly why they were doing what they were doing. The ANV marched from Virginia to Pennsylvania to an unheard beat of a drummer who remained silent about his plans.

R. E. Lee's counsel was his and his alone as he directed them toward a small town where something major had happened at the beginning of the American experiment in republican government. He was silent as he headed there to do a strange thing.

The Army of Northern Virginia followed Lee, though he was silent.

Was there a man dismay'd?
Not tho' the soldier knew
Some one had blunder'd:
Theirs not to make reply,
Theirs not to reason why,
Theirs but to do & die, ...[11]

Ultimately Lee's Northern invasion and the plan's collapse bore the rotting fruit of much destruction and social turbulence. The 1861 origin of the Confederate States of America consequently would not be reinforced; the collapsed plan could not draw attention to the November 1777 origin of the American nation as a government with a founding document. Inevitably, then, a proclamation of peace in the year 1863 at the seat of the 1777 United States government could not be made. As a result, for two more bloody years there was contentious existence *vis à vis* the Federal government and Southern people.

The catastrophic defeat of the Southern Confederation in 1865 would bewilder Southerners. They would have to drink a mixture of military and political, racial and financial poisons while on individual crucifixes of scorn for the North and suffering with their fellow Southrons. Their crosses would be devastating. Their flesh speared. Their spirits in a dry and barren land would have to swallow something more bitter than gall. Intellectual darkness at noon in the South, emotional darkness at night—except where white-hooded riders made it darker than midnight down in a cypress swamp.

General Pender did not live to see that specter as he wrote, "Everything seems to be going on finely. We might get to Phila. without a fight, I believe, if we choose to go. Gen. Lee intimates to no one what he is up to, and we can only surmise. ... This campaign will do one of two things: *viz*—to cause a speedy peace or a more tremendous war than we have had, the former may God grant."[12]

Ever since the day the young general wrote that letter, every interested person knows what followed the Northern Campaign was a "more tremendous war." In the two years after Lee's plan went awry at Gettysburg, there was decidedly un-speedy combat throughout the South as it sluggishly decayed in defeat.

There is something, however, we don't know: what God granted the South. We know it wasn't victory.

Lamentably General Pender died from wounds received at Gettysburg, not having looked upon a good scenario. Nor did he glimpse the bad one that actually happened in Dixie.

Thousands upon thousands of Southern soldiers died in the bad scenario. The dream of independence became the night terrors of William Tecumseh Sherman's March to the Sea. The march didn't stop at the Atlantic Ocean but turned northward and intensified greatly. South Carolina was punished mercilessly for its foolishness at Fort

Sumter, starting the war. Then came multiple skirmishes and hundreds of places of withdrawals, white flags, runaways, routs through North Carolina and into Virginia.

In the home state he sought to serve, Lee surrendered with Gethsemane-like suffering, more impaled by himself than by General U. S. Grant who, magnificent in respect for Lee and his troops, sent wagonloads of rations for the starving remnant of the once mighty Army of Northern Virginia. But it was only a pitiable remnant while a pathetic Confederate government fled from the police, scattering like thieves in the night.

Men like Jefferson Davis, John Reagan, all Cabinet officers, even some generals gutted out, hardly exemplifying their Constitution's call to "establish justice, insure domestic tranquility, secure the blessings of liberty, invoking the favor of Almighty God." Their dastardly charade of a virtuous government imploded while General Lee and General Joseph E. Johnston and others stayed at their posts and sought the welfare of their anguished men, facing the judgments of losing a war.

The political farce of Secession concluded with the downfall of the second Confederacy. The South's "peculiar institution" of slavery ended. The South's parochial view of "states rights" dissolved. The South collapsed since General Lee's attempt to *proclaim to the inhabitants that all we desire is PEACE, not conquest*" had not come to pass back on Independence Day, the Fourth of July 1863. Rain happened. Retreat happened.

Defeat and downpour. As if the ancient god of war, Mars, were punishing the South. Or, for all Southern Christians with primitive cultic beliefs about the Lord of Hosts, the Lord of Armies, their tribalistic god had withdrawn support.

Like all-things-Lee, the defeat, too, was a secret for weeks. But people did talk about rain. They thought rain was good, saving their retreating army since it bogged down the pursuing Federal army. The secret of the defeat became clear when ordinary soldiers wrote or trickled back home and told the story to people who had not heard. As well, the soldiers could only guess and speculate what they had been doing in the Northern Campaign. They must have been surprised—NO! flabbergasted—to learn that they *"had not been intended to fight a general battle ... unless attacked."* That is, *if* they ever did hear of Lee's official report of the general battle they had had to fight at Gettysburg, and then escape under the cover of rain.

The pathetic attempt to find something in that disastrous venture so as to justify more combat smacked of arrogance, smothered in ignorance. Pride went before a fall. Instead of surrender, the failing Confederacy chose two more years of disaster through combat.

Then the Confederacy had to count human loss: dead fathers, brothers, sons—thousands of them. Not to mention thousands more of uncles, nephews, cousins, friends, neighbors strewn on battlefields across Dixie in those two years after the Northern Campaign ended at Gettysburg.

Secrecy did not help Lee's effort for peace. Had his troops realized what they were fighting for in his Northern Campaign—a final attempt to end the war and save their lives—they well might have excelled Yankee Bluecoat valor at Gettysburg.

Secrecy hurt.

Secrecy killed.

Chapter Notes

1. Elizabeth Brown Pryor, Reading The Man (N.Y.: Viking, 2007): 356.
2. Jones, A Rebel War Clerk's Diary (Phila.: Lippincott, 1866): Vol II. 249.
3. Ibid. Vol. I. 375.
4. Ibid. I. 371.
5. Ibid. I. 373.
6. Ibid. I. 374.
7. WR:OR. I. 27. 2. 608
8.   WR:OR. I. 27. 2. 325.
9. William Dorsey Pender. The General To His Lady. Ed., W. H.

Hassler. (Chapel Hill, N.C.: University of N.C. Press, 1965):185. (Emphasis added)

10. Ibid. 247.
11. The Charge of The Light Brigade. Alfred, Lord Tennyson.
12. Pender. To His Lady. 253.

CHAPTER 11

"An Army Without Its Supply Train Is Lost"*

* *The Art of War,* Part VII "Maneuvering" Point 11 – Sun Tzu

ANOTHER PRECIOUS NUGGET about Lee's purpose has been in view for a century and a half but has not been taken seriously, if considered at all. Treated as devoid of military consequence for his Northern Campaign, this nugget is cast aside by writers and historians, as if tiny particles have only tiny value.

Benjamin Franklin long ago penned the wisdom that little things matter, some greatly: "For want of a nail the shoe was lost; for want of the shoe the horse was lost; for want of the horse, the rider was lost; for want of the rider the message was lost; for want of the message the battle was lost; for want of the battle the kingdom was lost!"

It may have been the case that Southern troops—and officers— didn't think cutting off a supply train was dangerous. Such thinking would have been as stupid as the severance itself.

The invading general informed his Commander-in-Chief, President Davis, on 25 June 1863—a mere six days before what would become the greatest battle of the war—that he had cut off his own supply lines when invading the enemy's homeland. In his usual manner of reasoned downplay, Lee wrote to Davis:

You will see that apprehension for the safety of Washington [D.C.] and their own territory has aroused the Federal government and people to great exertions, and it is incumbent upon us to call forth all our energies ... I have not sufficient troops to maintain my communications [supply lines] and, therefore, have to abandon them.[1]

Isn't it the case that if one is planning a great general battle to win a war, an invading general doesn't sever his own supply lines? *For whatever reason?* It's just not done. Had General Dwight Eisenhower cut off his supply lines six days before D-Day, June 1944, *for whatever reason,* he would have been relieved of command, without question. Probably summarily dismissed. Possibly court-marshaled. Or worse.

Robert Lee thought he had a reason. It was apparently a secret reason, not told to his chief lieutenants. He must have believed his reason was absolutely compelling. In war, isn't peace the highest reason for any action? For some reason Lee must have expected it would be self-evident that he wasn't going to fight a *general battle unless attacked,* and therefore would not need the supply system to be kept operative without materiel.

Such an act, self-evidently, could doom him in a general battle if there were to be one. Undeniably—even on a peace mission of some sort—if things went awry, a severed supply line could make the mission impossible to complete. And, whether he forgot the truth or ever knew it *per se* does not matter. What matters is that he missed a great truth about an army: "without provisions it is lost; without bases of supply it is lost," as General Sun Tzu wrote. There isn't any question but that in the summer of '63 R. E. Lee had a giant goal, yet seemed not to realize a giant goal can be a giant illusion. That grievous error resulted in a terrible conclusion.

The desire for peace will do that to people—even generals—since peace is such an overwhelming desire in wartime. In Lee's own words he was *not* going North to fight a general battle, unless attacked. He was *not* traveling through enemy territory for some 170 miles from the Maryland-Pennsylvania Mason-Dixon line eastward to Philadelphia without military supplies, as that would have been a recipe for sure disaster. He did not intend to wreak havoc on that big industrial center of the Union no matter what his officers may have imagined.

Nor was he going eastward through Pennsylvania, to then head south to Baltimore, some seventy miles away, without military supplies since Charm City was shielded by Union troops. Certainly he was *not* going to attack Washington from the north; that action would cause him to face massive numbers of people, military and civilian, who would have time to rush to Washington's defense while he meandered for 100 miles through southcentral Pennsylvania and northeastern Maryland.

No fool Lee. Stupid for cutting off his supply line, yes. But no fool to travel long distances—without resupply.

It was bad enough having to use troops to herd and protect the 60,000 head of livestock commandeered from Pennsylvania farmers and sent back to Virginia. Lee held no idea of going farther than Franklin, Adams, or York Counties in Pennsylvania. The southcentral counties of the Quaker State were the target of a *surpassing* raid which would climax with the special purpose of proclaiming peace at a special place.

Lee's calculation in mid-May, at the planning sessions in Richmond, that the Northern army would *not* pursue him was, unfortunately, a calculation based on wishful thinking. He convinced himself that the Northern army would fall back around Washington, D.C. to protect its national capital as it had done previously. Wishes are fairy tales for children, not for adults, explicitly not for adults who must make life-or-death decisions for thousands of people.

His assumption that the Union army would fall back again to protect Washington was reasonable, as Lee implied in his 25 June 1863 communication with Davis. General Lee miscalculated from the past, as do many; not enough of the past flows into the present to give precision to deductions about what is. Almost no precise deductions from the past can be made about what will be in the future. Lee's military calculus failed to include a political element: the President of the United States of America.

When the Army of Northern Virginia moved in June 1863, the politician Abraham Lincoln gave a direct military order in his role as Commander-in-Chief. He told the commanding general of the Federal Army of the Potomac, "Lee's army, not Richmond, is your sure [true] objective." The order was obeyed. Abraham Lincoln discerned the best way to defend Washington was to confront Lee's army wherever it was.

Subsequently a general battle would have to be fought, contrary to Lee's plan to proclaim peace. R. E. Lee had thought, all along, he wouldn't have to fight that battle. Nevertheless a battle came sneaking up on him unannounced.

With the Army of Northern Virginia in Pennsylvania, and its supply base in Staunton, Virginia, it should have been as obvious as the sky above—to someone in the ANV, one would think—that some needed materiel would be in limited supply. Certainly ammunition. Lee's men couldn't gather ammunition from the Pennsylvania area populace the way they had collected livestock and foodstuffs. Even if they had offered Northern greenbacks in place of Southern script, promising payment after the war, there wasn't shot nor shell to be had in farmers' barns. Cannon balls were out of the question. Everyone seems to have forgotten that "liberated" cattle, horses, and swine don't fight.

This rather unacknowledged stupid mistake meant the army without its supply train was lost—before the battle began. Nonetheless, the mistaken action is a precious particle that indicates Robert Lee planned something *other than* a mother-of-all-battles to deliver a knock-out blow to the Union.

R. E. Lee did plan something unusual, something that would surprise Abraham Lincoln if the plan could be actualized. The whole North, in Lee's analysis and rationalization, would see his action as more important than Lincoln's Proclamation, freeing Southern slaves.

General Lee would make his own proclamation, a small one, but one big in consequence. It would occur on an important day of national remembrance, a day steadily approaching as his army made its way North. It would occur at a special place in southcentral Pennsylvania.

And Heaven help him if he needed materiel from the supply line he had cut off.

Chapter Note

1. WR:OR. I. 27. 3. 931. Also see Steven E. Woodworth. Davis and Lee at War (Lawrence, KS: University Press of Kansas, 1995): 244-45 for an evaluation of Lee cutting off his supply line.

CHAPTER 12

"Many Things"—More Than Thought

UNDERGIRDING LEE'S PLAN was a singularly important point: "The key to victory was to sap the morale of the North."[1]

It was a point so important that Confederate military leaders saw its truth clearly.

"[T]he war had advanced far enough for us to see that a mere victory without decided fruits was a luxury we could not afford. Our numbers were less than the Federal forces, and our resources were limited while theirs were not. The time had come when it was imperative that the skill of generals and the *strategy and tactics* should take the place of muscle against muscle. Our purpose should have been to impair the *morale* of the Federal army and shake Northern confidence in the Federal leaders. We talked on that line from day to day, and General Lee accepted it as a good military view, adopted it as the key-note of the (Northern) campaign.[2]

Robert Lee was an astute observer of the human condition and understood that the only rational way the South could win, through war, its independence from the United States of America was by a quick loss of Northern support for the war.

He assessed the situation agriculturally, industrially, physically, militarily, numerically. Lee concluded that without an adequate navy to protect a much longer coastline than the North's, the South could not gain its goal unless it employed a massive psychological devise to undermine the morale of the Northern public.

After the victory at Fredericksburg in December 1862 he wrote his son, Brigadier General G. W. Custis Lee, that only a "revolution" against Lincoln's administration by the Union populace would stop the North's war against the South.[3]

Robert E. Lee knew the obvious truth: Southern arms would not be able to overcome Union forces. Any sensible person knew it was true; all except Southern hotspurs, warhawks. Those misguided half-intellects thought the Southern armies were Gideon's army of old, an army culled down to a few "true believers" who could conquer overwhelming armies.[4] Instead, Lee grasped that something momentous had to be devised which would cause Northern citizens to overthrow the Lincoln administration and stop the war.

Swiftly after his next victory, Chancellorsville in May 1863, Lee wrote to President Davis tendering an invitation to view that battlefield. The *good* reason he gave was, "I should be delighted if your health and convenience suited if you could visit the army. I could get you a comfortable room in the vicinity … and I know you would be content with our camp [food.]"

But the *real* reason behind the *good* reason for the invitation was, "There are many things about which I would like to consult Your Excellency."[5] A trial balloon from a commanding general would pique any commander-in-chief's interest, especially after two victories that had not tipped the scales for the end of hostilities.

After those dominating victories Lee was reluctant to project further victory because of the South's incapacities. In a letter to J. Davis on 10 June 1863, before Gettysburg, he wrote down his dire evaluation:

Conceding to our enemies the superiority claimed by them in numbers, resources, and all the means and appliances for carrying on the war, we have no right to look for exceptions from the military consequences of a rigorous use of those advantages [by them], excepting by such deliverances as the mercy of Heaven may accord the courage of our soldiers, the justice of our cause, and the constancy and prayers of our people. ... (I)t is nevertheless the part of wisdom to *carefully measure and husband our strength*, and not to expect from it more than ... it is capable of accomplishing. We should not, therefore, conceal from ourselves that our resources in men are *constantly diminishing* and the disproportion ... between us and our enemies ... is steadily *augmenting*. The *decrease* of the [size] of this army shows that the ranks are growing weaker and that its losses are not supplied by recruits. Under these circumstances we should *neglect no honorable means* of dividing and weakening our enemies. ... It seems to me that the most effectual mode of accomplishing this object, now within our reach, is to give all the *encouragement* we can consistently with truth, to the *rising peace party in the North*. ... Should the belief that peace will bring back the Union become general, the *war will no longer be supported* [up North], and that, **after all**, is what we're interested in bringing about. ... I think you will ... agree with me that we should at least carefully abstain from measures or expressions that tend to discourage any party whose purpose is peace.[6]

From battlefield victory to battlefield victory Robert Edward Lee was thinking of final victory: peace. There isn't evidence that he thought a third battlefield victory would turn the trick in the South's favor. Peace would have to come some other way.

His next move, after he realized that military action *per se* would not attain the goal of independence, depended on a special motive to revolutionize the Northern populace. "It is plain to my understanding that everything that will tend to repress the war feeling in the Federal States will inure to our benefit."[7]

In fact there was one issue huge enough to revolutionize the

South. The North, too. One issue was sufficiently important to sap the morale of the North, and to reinvigorate the South at the same time.

Abraham Lincoln had started it; he forced the South's hand—the North's, too.

Lincoln's *Emancipation Proclamation* stirred more than a whacked hornet's nest with its thousands of furious critters flitting about ready to attack anything and everything. Southerners were stung badly by the audacity of the document. Northerners reacted with anxiety to the social reach of the document, and were stung, also.

President Davis' reaction was fierce and extreme. He considered the Proclamation an endgame move: "A restitution of the Union has been rendered forever impossible," he thundered in a message to the Confederate Congress. He followed it with fire-breathing language of the direst kind: The Emancipation Proclamation is "the most execrable measure recorded in the history of guilty men" with "profound contempt for the impotent rage which it discloses" and "all commissioned officers of the United States army that hereafter may be captured ... may be dealt with ... the laws of the States providing for the punishment of criminals engaged in exciting servile insurrection."[8] Jefferson Davis "lost it," in modern parlance. So then it is no wonder at all that the Confederate Congress rejected his proposal!

Rebel war clerk Jones remonstrated bitterly on 15 January 1863 just after the document went into effect: "The Emancipation Proclamation, if not revoked, may convert the war into a most barbarous conflict."

Previously on 30 September 1862, a bit after President Lincoln had published his intention to promulgate the document on New Year's Day, 1863, Jones had noted the extent of the horrible bitterness of Southern leaders: "Lincoln's proclamation was the subject of discussion in the senate yesterday. Some of the gravest senators favor the raising of the *black flag*, asking and giving no quarter hereafter." (Emphasis in original)

The *black flag* in Western culture has been the political sign of destruction and death, of anarchy and nihilism. Some Southerners wanted to go that route, terrorizing and ravaging with brutality by night-riders, alarms, hooded thugs, dread, guerrilla raids, intimidation, and unmitigated fear behind the lines, in order to protect what they called their "Christian civilization"—one based on human slavery.

Even non-slave owners—the overwhelming majority of Southerners—were riled up about emancipation. That agitation spurred a magical impetus for Southern independence, inasmuch as Lincoln was messing with their pocketbooks. In a capitalist culture the most sensitive "nerve" in the whole body, speaking metaphorically, is the personal pocketbook nerve. That is, hit someone in the pocketbook and you'll hear a scream of "Bloody Murder." *Ergo* Lincoln was attacking and undermining the financial structure of the South and its predominant dependency on unpaid slave labor—of about four million black slaves living among a population of about eight million free white people.

That financial issue had an impact on the South far greater and more disturbing than the old political slogan, "The Union as it was and the Constitution as it is." That slogan was an abstract statement; it came from the past and framed slavery as a traditional political matter, but the slogan was more sound-and-fury than deed-and-action. However, it helped goad Southerners toward Secession. Slogans raise emotional heat but seldom produce intellectual light, and they become tiresome, to boot.

By mid-1863 that slogan was old hat. With Lincoln's Proclamation emancipating slaves in the rebellious states, the financial issue became a hard-core pocketbook issue. Monetary loss would be calamitous. Even more, the Proclamation would magnify a new catchphrase powerfully focusing on the poverty of most Southrons: "*A rich man's war and a poor man's fight.*"

That slogan dated from earlier in the war but Lincoln's Proclamation intensified the difference between the poorer non-plantation class of the South and the landed plantation class. The former group would suffer wage-depression because freed slaves would undercut them by working for mere pennies, while the landlords would remain on the top rung, getting rich. The Proclamation had the power to undermine the Confederate economy drastically, thus the war effort would suffer to the same degree.

By the year after Lee's failed Northern Campaign, with the high point of the Confederate war effort past, that popular mantra about money matters had become so entrenched in Southern consciousness that it was a low-grade fever, politically speaking. It described accurately the ordinary Southerner's sickening plight.

The War Department's J. B. Jones recorded incident after incident of financial favoritism. For example, "Over 100,000 landed proprietors, and most of the slaveowners, are now out of the ranks, and soon, I fear we shall have an army that will not fight. ... And this is the result of the pernicious policy of partiality and exclusiveness ... the *higher* class staying home and making money, the *lower* class thrust into the trenches."[9]

Of critical significance Jones recorded that the commanding general saw the situation clearly: "Gen. Lee writes urgently for *more men* ... and he complains that rich young men are elected [local] magistrates, etc., just to avoid service in the field."[10] The pathetic situation was, "The poor men in the army (the rich are not in it) can get nothing for their families and there is the prospect of their families starving."[11]

In a predictive mood, Jones wrote, "I look for other and more disastrous defeats, unless the speculators are demolished, and the wealthy class put in the ranks. ... The lagging land proprietors, slaveowners, as the Yankees shrewdly predicted, want to be captains, etc., or speculators. The poor will not long fight for their oppressors, the money changers, extortioners, etc., whose bribes keep them out of the service."[12] On and on Jones' plaint went, decrying the rich man's war and the poor man's fight: "The government must not crush the spirit of the people relied upon for defense, and the rich must fight side by side with the poor, or the poor will abandon the rich, and that will be the abandonment of the cause."[13] The Southern home front was deteriorating.

Dreadfully high inflation continued to soar throughout Dixie. Rebellious events escalated; army desertions bulked large in all Southern armies, including the army of their greatest general, Robert E. Lee. Home-front food riots materialized, usually led by soldiers' wives left to fare for themselves, along with other starving mothers and children. Troops on the front lines repeated often, "Rich man's war; poor man's battle," even as they griped bitterly about poor officers or slaveowners exempt by law from military service. The catchphrase became ubiquitous. Money shouted._

On the other hand, the *lack* of money roared. And when it had to do with taking away the wealth—emancipating slaves—then the roar turned to howls of dismay. Resentfully, the *lack* of money complained, cursed, then threatened to perpetuate the same severe action it had provoked in 1863, in the bombardment by hot-heads at Fort Sumter in '61: warfare of the undeclared kind.

At its outset, the war's success seemed assured—with top-grade officers from West Point in their Southern armies. Then followed inspired farmers, tradesmen, craftsmen, seeming to predict an easy war for the South and a quick victory.

And such expectations soon collapsed. Years of suffering—poverty, preferential treatment for the wealthy, infighting among political leaders professing noble goals, rampant financial exploitations, near-starvation of troops—wrought havoc throughout Dixieland. Soldiers were plagued with terrible desertion rates by their comrades-in-arms while they were left barefooted, underfed and undersupplied, yet constrained to fight for the cause those others had abandoned. On the home front living costs spiraled upward daily, state governments fought with the central government in Richmond, and some states threatened to secede from secession! The cause of independence for whites and slavery for blacks was monstrously unequal—and now a piece of paper by a Northern president was going to destroy the euphemistic "peculiar institution" and supposedly everything Southern.

Lincoln's emancipation effort, through the Proclamation, could readily end in failure since it was a presidential, not a congressional, directive. Such failure would have been a major defeat for the Northern cause. Southerners thought the war and slavery were not only socially proper and necessary but divinely ordained and righteous. In Dixie money had everything to do with slavery; one dared not touch the "peculiar institution." If that institution were changed, everything would collapse. Southern economic wealth was singularly reliant on slavery, yet since the founding of the Republic in 1777, it was wealth always under question and attack. The cry, "Cotton is King" was true only because slave labor made it the economic backbone of the South. In fact, before the war "the nation's twelve richest counties all lay in the South, a region that constituted on its own the fourth largest economy in the world."[14] Cotton was grown in those twelve counties as successfully as digital paraphernalia flourish today in Silicon Valley California.

Yet those breakaway states didn't have substantial railroad systems to speak of, primarily because the tracks they had nearly always ran from plantations to coastal ports. They were without substantial ore mines, plentiful fishing ports, or sufficient factories to produce consumer goods in large quantities. The South was not, overall, a wealthy region at the beginning of the Industrial Revolution in America.

But it had slaves. Four million of them. And it had cotton. Slaves plant; slaves pick cotton. Most every Southerner thought it all was good—and all from God. The whole system was God-blessed, and therefore, righteous.

Of course, such hyper-rationalization was self-righteous. But some Southerners considered self-righteousness good: it had something "righteous" in it by definition! Decidedly, Southern theology was not well thought through. Emancipation of slaves, manifestly, was evil to the Southern mind-set. Therefore, independence from the Union was the only route the Confederacy could take to keep slavery viable. Of course, independence meant war, continued war—possibly *continual* war. And all because of "The Devil," Abraham Lincoln, who was thought dead wrong about emancipating slaves. And should be dead himself!

Northerners, on the other hand, were stunned by Lincoln's Proclamation.

Relative to that point in time, another precious particle of historical gold has come down to us, one that likely pleased Robert E. Lee immensely. Shockingly, the Pennsylvania House of Representatives in April 1863 passed a resolution calling the Emancipation Proclamation by Mr. Lincoln "unwise, unconstitutional, and void" in its entirety. Also, the state Assembly Representatives *demanded* a convention of the States to end the war.[15] Few people would question that Robert Lee would have read this Pennsylvania development in the newspapers. Such information would make his plan for the Pennsylvania Campaign well reasoned, therefore all the more feasible, practical.

Many Northerners—almost as many as down South—were opposed to equality with the Negro in any way, at any time, in any place. But the many had to contend with the Abolitionists, an extremely active group of Northerners growing daily, advocating freeing the slaves. Pivotally, Abolitionists were politically astute, articulate and active, easily making them the more important group, consequently, the more powerful group, up North.

In a different form of self-righteousness, Abolitionists lambasted anyone who didn't join their effort to fully free all slaves everywhere, immediately. They insisted they were right. They insisted that slaves must be freed everywhere, in *all* the States, during the year of the Emancipation Proclamation—not freed only in the States in rebellion to which Lincoln restricted the Proclamation. They castigated President Lincoln for moderating emancipation of black slaves throughout the country.

A Northern split, or splits, over slavery and emancipation could be helpful to General Lee's plan. He would counteract emancipation with something greater. And the counteraction would propose a more universal human goal: peace for South and North.

Lee's agenda in May 1863 included "many things" to discuss with Jefferson Finis Davis. Those "many things" were coalescing into a plan to erode Northern morale, to undercut the North's commitment to the war, and to end the war in the year Abraham Lincoln wanted to end slavery, for some slaves.

His *wisest, grandest, most imposing scheme* entailed behind the scene matters that were operative the Spring of '63. No doubts about it, the alert and rational Robert Edward Lee could incorporate them effectively into his plans for Southern independence. Indeed, there were "many things" General Lee wanted to talk over with President Davis.

More things than had been thought about previously.

More than were thought through.

Chapter Notes

1. Pryor. Reading The Man. 388.
2. General James Longstreet, "Lee's Invasion of Pennsylvania" in Battles and Leaders of the Civil War (N.Y.: Castle Books reprint,1983): Vol. 3. 247.
3. Clifford Dowdey and Louis H. Manarin (eds.) The Wartime Papers of R. E. Lee (Boston: Little, Brown, 1961): 411.
4. Holy Bible (AV). Judges, chap. 7.
5. WR/OR. I. 25. 2. 783.
6. WR/OR. I. 27. 3. 881-82. (Emphases added)
7. WR/OR. I. 27. 3. 930.
8. A. C. Bancroft. The Life and Death of Jefferson Davis, Ex-President of the Southern Confederacy (N.Y.: Ogilvie Publishers,1889): 27.
9. Jones. Rebel War Clerk's Diary. 2. 281. (Emphasis in original)
10. Ibid. (Emphasis in original)
11. Ibid. 2. 284.
12. Ibid. 2. 288.
13. Ibid. 2. 368.
14. Tony Horwitz. Midnight Rising: John Brown and The Raid That Sparked the Civil War. (N.Y.: Holt, 2011): 37.
15. Arnold Shankman, The Pennsylvania Anti-War Movement 1861-1865 (London: Associated University Press):1980. 113.

CHAPTER **13**

Splinters and Pickings

THE EMANCIPATION PROCLAMATION could have split off the seceded states irrevocably, no question about it. And worse was on the
horizon.

By late 1862—after President Lincoln announced his Emancipation
Proclamation was to become effective 1 January 1863 and before
the battle of Gettysburg—some states *north* of the Mason-Dixon Line
could have split off, also. Some could have sided with the South to
the degree of joining the Confederacy, as a legislator in Pennsylvania
proposed. Other Northern states could have split off to become independent, holding other particular sets of prejudices along racial or
social lines, some pro-immigrant or anti-immigrant, or along lines financial or political, anti-Roman Catholic or pro-Roman Catholic. Or,
the whole war could have ended in defeat for the North, and states
would have scattered.

The chance was slight, yet there was the possibility everything
would be tattered and shattered up North: families, businesses, social
institutions, churches and synagogues, governance, waffling states,
ideals, national history, the Republic itself.

All the while, France had troops on the southwestern border of the
United States and had established a government in Mexico. It was a
scenario more problematic than twenty-first-century Americans might
think. It violated the unilaterally propagated "Monroe Doctrine"—
and making the situation even knottier was the Southern flirtation

with becoming Mexican! The Rebel war clerk indicates the situation in its freakishness:

> The news from Mexico is refreshing our people. The 'notables' of the new government under the auspices of the French General, Forey have proclaimed the [Mexican] States an Empire, and offered the throne to Maximilian of Austria … Our people, *very many of them*, just at this time, *would not object being included* in the same Empire. [1]

Southern aristocracy thought itself true-blue, the blood of royalty in its veins. Aristocrats paid attention to human bloodlines as if they were pedigree horseflesh; they traced their families back to "old Europe" to determine which royal line they inherited. Many thought they deserved royal titles and trappings. Both prizes for Southern aristocrats were just south of the border.

Since royalty is the forerunner of the modern celebrity, many war-weary Southerners felt refreshed with the possibility of being well known, celebrated. It seemed an invitation was just around the corner, ready to be tendered to Southern white aristocrats to become dukes and duchesses, even lowly baronets and baronesses. Many wouldn't object to being included—Southern drawls and black servants, corn pone and black-eyed peas, too.

In those same years the United Kingdom maintained a strong British presence in an outpost nation to the north of America—remembering well the loss of the lower thirteen colonies in 1783.

In 1863 the UK remembered not only 1783, but the War of 1812, too, which America started with a declaration of war. When the invading British Army advanced into Washington, D. C.—under a flag of truce to discuss terms of surrender—it was fired upon by an armed group of citizens in a home at the intersection of Constitution Avenue, Maryland Avenue, and Second Street. The British were rattled by the attack on the flag of truce by the zealots and retaliated by burning the capital city.

They destroyed the two Houses of Congress (the Rotunda not yet under construction) and the U. S. Treasury building, but helped save the U. S. Patent Office for its wealth of material! Luckily, a thunderstorm with violent rains from a hurricane saved some public buildings from complete destruction. It dampened other fires, as well, yet spun-off a small tornado that ruined a section of the city. The White House was gutted by fire, but Dolley Madison stayed long enough to place some of the dinner silverware in a fine silk handbag with wrist straps, before she escaped— and made ice cream, according to legend.

The mayor of Alexandria, Virginia across the river from the capital made a deal with the British not to burn his town. No one ever talked about how much money changed hands.

During the war the British with their trusted Maple Leaf partners north of the border repulsed three different American attacks on Canada. America was almost on its knees, but some victories on Lake Eire saved the nation.

Finally England had to withdraw its troops. For good reason: its nemesis Napoleon Bonaparte was setting his forces to invade England a few miles across the Channel. The United Kingdom couldn't stay in its former colonies to defeat them—or even reclaim them in that war. The French again saved America as it did earlier at Yorktowne in the Revolutionary War, although it was not intentional this time. The British Bulldog had to get back home to save merry olde England from Bonaparte.

The peace Treaty of Ghent, between England and America in 1814, released England to confront Napoleon. Significantly, the treaty had returned *everything* to the way it was before that war! The treaty did not formally stop the impressment of American seamen off American ships—even some warships—because the British contended certain American sailors were really British citizens.

Psychologically, the Battle of New Orleans—fought *after* the peace treaty had already been signed—left a good taste in America's mouth but didn't do anything to end the *already ended* war. "Rule, Britannia! Britannia, rule the waves," as in 1812, still sounded foreboding in

1863, sounding out of the British Province of Canada farther up north.

The Southern interest with foreign absorption got complex; it smothered the good sense still surviving down South. "A writer in the [Richmond] *Sentinel* suggests if we should be hard pressed the [Confederate] States ought to repeal the old Declaration of Independence, and voluntarily revert to their original proprietors—England, France, and Spain—and by them be protected from the North."[2] Wars often are started by madmen, and are just as often continued by other lunatics. The South was not an exception, at all.

Repeal the *Declaration of Independence*? What demon possessed some Southerns? All to protect slavery! Give up the quest for independence only to become subject to foreign monarchs? Again? What about "states' rights" after rejoining the English Empire? Madness was slithering through Dixieland.

Commonly when division takes place in political thoughts another takes place: sub-division. Secessionist action breeds proliferations. Politics learns a terrible lesson from religions which, when they splinter, splinter on and on and on, near endlessly. In the process they give up much independence, freedom they thought they'd get. Instead they get an amorphous, corrupted miscellany which they call a rationale; and so, so "fore-damned they sit, to each his [own] priest and whore," as Rudyard Kipling wrote in *Tomlinson*.

Sheer, unadulterated madness was erupting like boils across the South. It is no wonder the war clerk wrote, "We breakfast, dine, and sup on horrors now, and digest them all sullenly."[3]

America, North and South, was ripe for collapse from internal splintering. Ripe for pickings by external powers, also. The possibility of the war ending in defeat hovered over both South and North. The specter of easy pickings by other nations hung low on the horizon.

Chapter Notes

1. Jones. Rebel War Clerk's Diary. I. 391-92. (Emphasis added)
2. Ibid. II. 355.
3. Ibid. II. 361.

CHAPTER 14

A Novel, a Document, a Piece of Music*

* (*The Art of War* Again)

TWO MASSIVE PROPAGANDA documents sprang from Northern soil fully bloomed and vividly colored, like nothing before in American history. The South had nothing to compare—or contrast—with them; it was overwhelmed emotionally by both.

The first, *Uncle Tom's Cabin: Or Life Among the Lowly,* was a work of fiction by Harriet Beecher Stowe. Like all art, according to Pablo Picasso, it was "a lie that makes us realize truth, at least the truth that is given us to understand." The events of the book didn't happen as such but the book portrayed a frank image of man's inhumanity to man, that is, of white people to black people in the antebellum South.

The novel was published in 1852 in Mrs. Stowe's response to the nefarious Fugitive Slave Act of 1850. That legislation practically committed every American citizen—Northerner, Southerner, Easterner, or Westerner—to be a legal deputy of the government to catch runaway slaves. The law itself was long and vindictive in tone, wicked in its intent to make everyone a tool of the state, heinous because it denied runaway slaves the right to speak on their own behalf or to be tried before a jury of any sort. And more, it was diabolical in making people opposed to slavery actually serve the interests of owners of human beings as property. Enough Northern congressmen had agreed to passage of the law to keep the South from breaking up the

Federal Union in 1850, but they only delayed the inevitable divisive acts of the people who hated the America of the United States.

The South loathed every word of Stowe's book. The North believed every word of the book as truth, whether literally or figuratively.

Mrs. Stowe's novel didn't titillate or thrill the public. Its message simply simmered—no, boiled!—for nine years, evangelizing Abolitionism almost as a state religion in New England. Its gospel spread ever wider over the Northern states and into the Far West. The message was clear: Slaves, though black, are human beings and human beings must be free from chains that symbolize their status as property.

The ramification of the message was clearer to the South than the North. The end of Southern culture, what there was of it, was at hand along with its financial underpinnings.

The other massively important document of the North was a work of public pleading. Sheer political defiance in time of war, it was written by Abraham Lincoln. The Emancipation Proclamation boiled over—no, exploded—on the political landscapes, both North and South, in late 1862 and early 1863.

Up North the Proclamation had a civic stamp of approval that provided both legality and morality to its message. By implication, it had a religious imprimatur, too, furnishing a sort of scriptural authority that no novel has ever had.

Many quickly framed the Proclamation as if it were a Heavenly commandment issued from the mountaintop of the Federal Government itself. It took two years, but Lincoln got God on the side of the North.

The Proclamation had persuasive power, a political dynamism that moved rational beings. More—much more—the Proclamation also had a convincing religious fervor that moved people passionately, *pro* or *contra*. Its passion was expressed as if it were music, like the striding, sweeping songs of patriotism or the exuberant, marching hymns of the Kingdom of God.

Music can do that to people. It is a way of interpreting reality just as valid as is clear description of life's actualities or mathematical accuracy. Music is primeval, in truth it is embryonic—with much yet to come forth. Quoth Shakespeare: *as they say, from iron came music's origin.*

Music is a mystery whose soul searching and personality changing can neither be described adequately nor explained thoroughly. Its merit is that it is capable of moving human beings—and human mountains of indecisiveness, doubt, fear, even opposition.

And music lasts. Through days and years, through hard times and good times. It lasts into future times; music's power survives.

Germans sing about its timelessness:

Himmel und Erde müssen vergeh'n
Heaven and earth must pass away;

Aber die Musici, aber die Musici.
Only music, only music.

Aber die Musici bleibt besteh'n.
Only music will remain.

Music was by no means a small factor for the North during the war. "The Battle Hymn of the Republic" was the power that solidified Northern steel and zeal in the face of divisiveness at home and rebellion away from home. That song was a musical rendition of the Emancipation Proclamation. It swept the North. It swept aside the South, ultimately.

Wartime music for the South had a jumbled value. "Robert E. Lee once listened to a band concert in camp and said, *I don't see how we could have an army without music.*"[1] Even so, the music the South had was basically show tunes, riverboat melodies, sentimental ballads. None of them was known to induce patriotism in place of pleasure. Amusement and delight don't gel into home-front patriotism, military enlistments, or daily commitments; very little "iron" existed in such melodies.

Southern tunes were entertaining but never marching music like the French "Marseillaise" nor the reverent energy of England's "God Save the Queen." Songs such as "The Bonny Blue Flag" or "Dixie" did not invigorate the masses to action, clearly not to militant action; they did not fire up men to enlist or civilians to willingly sacrifice. Pleasing, indeed. Martial, minimally down to imaginary, such tunes did provide a respite to Southern troops and stirred love for their homes. However, something else was needed.

Southerners had to rely on a sound effect: the "Rebel Yell." Yet the yell was appropriate only during battle, having as much effect on the hearer as the howler, though the effects were opposite: fear and fortification.

It couldn't be used to recruit troops for the ranks, nor to encourage financing the war, nor to heighten patriotism of civilians. It was too blatant and overblown for Southern patricians and high society, too pseudomacho for the Southern self-image of gentility, that is, cultivated, decorous, and elegant. In recruitment, finances, or patriotic displays it was a non-starter for the yell cut out half the white people—women that is—and all the black people in the Southern states.

The reason for the yell's inability to foster patriotism any place except the battlefield can be stated categorically: The world does not gather where there is yelling. Hollering may wind up courage in combat but elsewhere it nails down anxiety as a permanent fixture in the human psyche.

Of the Northern songs none could compare favorably with the words of Julia Ward Howe's poem that she wrote hastily in the early morning twilight so as not to forget when daylight arrived. A friend had asked the previous day, "Why not write some good words for that stirring tune?" That is, William Steffe's dynamic tune, named "John Brown's Body." Northern troops picked it up quickly, singing it as they strode from place to place to do battle until it became an integral part of their intellectual and spiritual armory. Its primary words were:

John Brown's body lies a-mouldering in the grave …
He's gone to be a soldier in the Army of the Lord,
His soul goes marching on.

Mrs. Howe transposed them into:

Mine eyes have seen the glory of the coming of the Lord;
He is trampling out the vintage where
the grapes of wrath are stored;
He hath loosed the fateful lightning of his terrible swift sword; …
Glory! Glory! Hallelujah! His truth is marching on!
I have seen Him in the watch fires of a hundred circling camps …
Glory! Glory! Hallelujah! His day is marching on.
He has sounded forth the trumpet that shall never sound retreat …
Glory! Glory! Hallelujah! Our God is marching on.
In the beauty of the lilies Christ was born across the sea,
With a glory in his bosom that transfigures you and me;
As he died to make men holy let us die to make men free; …
Glory! Glory! Hallelujah. While God is marching on.

Howe had embedded Shakespeare's understanding that "from iron/came music's origin" into the poem's content and cadence so that they fit perfectly the high-power fervency of the lyrics: *John Brown's body lies a-mouldering in the grave.* "The Battle Hymn of the Republic"—then, and ever since.

The North had the best marching songs, period. "Tramp. Tramp. Tramp, the Boys are marching," "Rally Round The Flag, Boys," "We're Coming, Father Abraham," "John Brown's Body." A Southern major admitted to Northern officers after the war, "Gentlemen, if we'd had your songs, we'd have licked you out of your boots."[2]

One side in that war had music "from iron." It had vibrant, spirited, action-packed, emotion-moving, and intellect-grabbing tunes.

Martial music North and South was an uneven match from the get-go.

And Robert Lee, ever the astute general *qua* non-political politician, grasped the over-all public, political, and military situation: enthusiasm dwindling of the South side, growing on the North side. Something phenomenal had to be done for balance, to correct the differential. Differentials between South and North were significant, easily noted in population sizes, material resources, ideals, music, railroads, army sizes, education facilities, manufacturing, and just about every other category—except the élan of several, not all, Confederate armies.

There isn't a question that *esprit*, and flair, vivacity, zest, and pizzazz are good, and that a few Southern armies had them in abundance. Yet, as often as not, those good characteristics are not good enough! Throughout the South, élan <u>shown</u> brightest in the Army of Northern Virginia. All the same, something more than emotions was needed if the South truly wanted to win a protracted war.

After his retreat from the battle of Antietam/Sharpsburg, Maryland in September 1862—in the wake of which Lincoln speedily capitalized on the retreat, feeling free to announce his Emancipation Proclamation to take effect 1 January 1863—Robert E. Lee began to see a bigger picture. He foresaw the trouble the South would have counteracting that major and melodramatic initiative on Lincoln's part. There would be trouble to overcome the Lincolnian strategy but Lee thought the South still could win independence, *if* it had an awe-inspiring victory.

The victory would have to be unique, however. *Different*.

Since his two greatest victories at Fredericksburg and Chancellorsville did not diminish nor halt, but temporarily, the Northern Army of the Potomac, R. E. Lee knew categorically he had to devise a *different* strategy. A massive battle on enemy soil would—at best—be a repeat of those two military victories, victories which had not stopped the North in its tracks either in Virginia or Mississippi. Or anywhere else for that matter.

The victory would have to be something important enough to counterbalance the enemy's Emancipation Proclamation. It would have to "mystify, mislead, and surprise the enemy" in General Jackson's words.

Necessarily, then, it had to be super-political, above and beyond what had been done previously in the policy realm.

Of course it would have to be a military operation of sorts, a *surpassing* one, and somehow above and beyond what had been done in his previous significant victories at Fredericksburg and Chancellorsville. They were "successes" that didn't succeed; the enemy still was on Southern soil. Those battles cost him dearly in men and materiel and the North was still in Dixieland at many places. A third such battle, say one on enemy soil, might—but might not—be victorious.

Robert E. Lee was planning a *surpassing* effort of some kind. It would be psychological warfare at its best. Sun Tzu would have been proud of Robert Edward Lee. Sun Tzu could have used him as an example in *The Art Of War,* had Lee lived some two millennia before, in China.

Accordingly one should not wonder that Lee won big in December 1862 and again in May 1863. His troops had a "gut" dynamic to preserve their way of life as well as gain independence for the Confederate States of America. In the spring and summer of '63 his troops were ready to follow him to the gates of Hell itself—and on the attack, yet not to defend Southern soil. It was a polar opposite situation from his usual campaigns on Virginian soil. Maybe it was too antipodean, poles too far apart.

The Proclamation had whipped up a heady brew. It intoxicated the South into a drunk-like anger. Morally, it was hard liquor for many in the North, too, creating bitter animosities between people *pro* and people *contra* Lincoln's action. It sharply severed Abolitionists, who wanted all slaves freed, from most other people who wanted to staunch the rebellion militarily and not made a social issue a political issue, certainly not a military one. South and North were conscious that something impolitic—maybe wicked, maybe destructive—would result from the Emancipation Proclamation.

That document, in effect since New Year's Day 1863, surely was one of the *many things* R. E. Lee indicated to President Davis that he wished to consult him about after the amazing victory at Chancellorsville. The Proclamation's effect on Southern troops would be paramount, but the effects on public reaction would have important ramifications for the psychological warfare Lee was planning—both the *united* Southern public reaction to it, and the *divided* Northern public reactions to the document.

One of the *many things* Lee would have been expected Davis to consider was how Northern acceptance of the war could be changed radically by simply "maneuvering." Davis had used that word to signify a device, a tactic, a contrivance to oppose the Lincoln Administration's psychological act of "freeing" slaves in the rebel states, where Lincoln had no control.

What if it would be a Southern psychological counter-operation with some "*honorable* means of dividing and weakening our enemies," such as a peace proposal? [3]

What if Lee's effort at psychological warfare was to decipher that *"the supreme excellence in war is breaking the enemy's resistance without fighting"* as proposed in *The Art of War*, "Weak Points and Strong" Number 9 by the ancient Chinese General Sun Tzu. Such an effort would produce a Lee who would **not** *seek a general battle*—to break the enemy's resistance.

General Sun Tzu's treatise was introduced to the Western World in 1772 through a French translation by a Jesuit priest, Jean J. M. Amiot. That translation was influential in the writings of the military theorist Antoine-Henri Jomini, one of Napoleon's generals.

Bonaparte himself also had read and was influenced by Sun Tzu's *Art of War*.

Then Jomini's book, *Traité de grande tactique* (Treatise on Grand Military Operations) was published in English, in America, as *The Art of War* in 1854 by G. Putnam Broadway in New York. Jomini's works on military strategy were the *only* ones taught at West Point prior to The War of the Rebellion, so Confederate and Union officers educated at the United States Military Academy were imbued with French (and Chinese) strategies and tactics.

But of equal importance to its advent into American military schooling is the knowledge that R. E. Lee was fluent in French and took honors in that language while a student at West Point.

A priceless bit of historical gold comes down to us in a letter to his daughter Agnes, dated 6 February 1863. General Lee wrote that Federal General Joseph Hooker "is playing the *Chinese* game, trying what frightening will do. He runs out his guns, starts wagons and troops up and down the river, and creates an excitement generally." (Emphasis added)

Hooker-type operations was the "Chinese game" Sun Tzu wrote about in *The Art of War*, "Maneuvering" Point 20: "*Hold out baits to entice the enemy. Feign disorder, and* [then] *crush him.*" Hooker tried for three months to entice Lee before the battle of Chancellorsville, but there's little doubt that the Southern commander knew the principles of *The Art of War*. Lee knew about "Chinese fortune cookies." He wasn't biting.

The above facts, coupled with the knowledge that Jomini's *Art of War* was published in English during Lee's years as Superintendent of the Military Academy, 1852-55, send still another nugget of historical gold our way. R. E. Lee *may* have been cognizant early in his career of Sun Tzu's *The Art of War* in the French language. Lee *may* have had a seed planted about how to gain final victory in any given war. We do not know what he read or did not read—except that as a father he forbade the reading of novels by his children and, also, as West Point Superintendent he strongly spoke against military cadets reading novels! In his formative years there may have been a Chinese source for a precious particle that flowed down to the Southerner, and us, *via* France.

The idea of breaking the enemy's resistance by not fighting, by using some greater tactic, is *the supreme excellence in war*. Whatever its origin, General Lee sought to practice it in due time.

Inevitably, given Lee's propensity for action and some precious militarily strategic innovations, it makes sense that General Lee wanted to march out of Virginia. Heading North. Not to fight a general battle. To proclaim a peace proposal to outweigh and override the propaganda of the Emancipation Proclamation. To *break the enemy's resistance without fighting.*

It makes eminent sense—it is even, perhaps, wisdom—that Robert Lee would *"proclaim … PEACE"* on the Fourth of July in the year of his greatest victory at Chancellorsville. Equally wise, it seems, that a reflective intellect such as Lee would proclaim at a particular place in Pennsylvania, chosen for its historical value and therefore, its psychological impact.

Both *Uncle Tom's Cabin* and the Emancipation Proclamation had elicited a powerful response from the South's leading general, R. E. Lee: unheralded peace-seeker.

Chapter Notes

1. Burke Davis. The Civil War: Strange and Fascinating Facts (N.Y.: Fairfax Press, 1982): 45.
2. Geoffrey Ward. The Civil War: An Illustrated History (N.Y.: Knopf Borzoi, 1990): 104.
3. WR/OR. I. 27. 3. 881.

CHAPTER 15

Unfinished Business in Richmond

R. E. LEE was occupied with a quandary as much oversized as was the Union army still opposing him in Virginia in May 1863. Perhaps one even larger.

"Lee could not afford many more battles like Chancellorsville, which later he claimed left him 'more depressed than after Fredericksburg' [because] his army had prevailed at a cost that nearly cancelled out whatever tactical and operational benefit had been gained."[1] His military efforts had resulted in two victories; they did not accomplish what he wanted.

The next move of the Army of Northern Virginia would have been one of the "many things" about which Lee wanted to consult with President Davis, in the meeting Lee proposed. What plan of action would be feasible for future operations in the coming summer of 1863?

However, his attempt to speak privately, that is, to speak—on his own ground—to his constitutionally determined Commander-in-Chief, did not result in privileged consultations out in the field. Rather, meetings occurred in the Southern capital of Richmond because Jefferson Davis was unable to travel, and could not go to Lee. Illness rendered Davis vulnerable to the elements and duress of travel over country roads.

The upshot was the General's trip to the President instead. In Richmond Lee was unavoidably engaged in meetings over four days in May. Instead of spending time alone with Davis, Lee found himself in group meetings. It was unusual for one accustomed to face-to-face private meetings with the President or the Secretary of War.

Present at some meetings were President Davis and Secretary of War James Seddon. Other meetings included Davis, Seddon, and the senior general of the Confederacy, Samuel Cooper, Adjutant and Inspector General Confederate States Army. There were prolonged meetings with the Presidential Cabinet of five members, and possibly other meetings with some of the aforementioned top officials in attendance.

Since records of the meeting contents are nowhere to be found, precise information as to which participants were present when and where, the explicit topics discussed, agreements and/or disagreements articulated, exact decisions, and possible options discussed are all difficult to know. Thus, a cloud of obscurantism hangs over the meetings—downright suspicion that something inappropriate, even flawed, was in the works.

Daylong sessions—and at least one meeting long into the night—resulted. It has to be the case that such meetings were strenuous, if not deleterious, to the ill Chief Executive. Probably to others as well. Certainly one other attendant evinced displeasure at the results of the meetings. Conceivably General Lee, himself, was affected, feeling hamstrung by officials who didn't have to face the working end of rifle or cannon. Making decisions is usually difficult. It's easy, however, when compared—or contrasted—with having to make decisions surrounded by shot and shell on a battlefield.

It was a strange decision-making process for a professed military campaign. But meet they did, in plural numbers over plural days, with, it would seem, plural understandings of what General Lee proposed for the 1863 Summer Campaign of the Army of Northern Virginia.

Plainly, Robert Lee spoke in the meetings. How else could he present his swiftly formulated plan? As a strategist he surely spoke of the condition of his country and its people: their patriotism, or lack thereof, as seen in lowering numbers of volunteers and the increasing rate of desertions. He couldn't have failed to discuss the economics of having various armies in the field from the Atlantic Ocean to the Mississippi River, from the Gulf of Mexico to the Ohio River. He would have had to address the need to pressure the North into realizing it could not subdue the vast Southland, thus effectively ending the war. Probably he would opine about ways to inspire the populace.

Chiefly he'd speak of the government's efforts to bring the war to a successful conclusion; his goal as a soldier. The approach would be psychological, much more than martial, in tone.

The slightest of possibilities is that Lee had assembled a war room scenario. It was not his way of approaching authorities to throw at them graphic diagrams and illustrations, troop placements and strength, and routes of travel or movements. It was not his style. And to change his style for the civilians present, to what avail?

No. Lee would have relied upon forthright intellectual arguments, crafting rational concepts to guide his plan and then driving his concepts with the passionate gut desire to win in a righteous cause, all amalgamated to be an in-the-face action against the enemy. And on its soil.

Meshing intellectual argument with passionate desire would be a psychological effort that could gain approval. A coup if he could pull it off, in fact a *coup de maître,* masterful if he could convince civilian officials his unique plan could be pulled off successfully.

After making such an approach he probably would have returned to his quiet, stoic approach to problems. He would have listened, without questions or comments.

He would have to listen to politicians. And they would have talked and talked; that's what they're good at and the reason they got their jobs. They probably would have recounted the conditions of their own official portfolios, their departments' interests, including contacts with the public in order to keep people reconciled to and involved in the war effort.

Without fail the politicians would have broached the most important policy issue at hand: getting diplomatic recognition from England

and France. The South depended on foreigners coming to its aid. They thought, unrealistically, of trying to have both countries intervene in the war on behalf of the Confederacy, even though slavery was first abolished in France in 1794, then definitively abolished in 1848 and in England the Abolition Act of 1833 had done the same in the United Kingdom. Did Confederate leaders think those countries would get mixed up and messed up with slavery again? Half-backed ideas are mushy and sticky, like half-baked buns.

Chiefly, of course, Cabinet members would make the easy political play of lambasting the North. Such an approach could upgrade their "patriotic" creditability with President Davis.

The toll on the General Commanding, who was better acquainted with listening to his sub-commanders—followed by decisions as *fait accomplis*—can only be conjectured. Without question it couldn't have been a joyful experience for an active field commander. Truthfully put, such encounters may actually have inhibited Lee from adequately clarifying his purpose and plan for their civilian consumption.

For whatever reason, the Cabinet was not clearly understanding what was to happen. Perhaps the same could be said about General Cooper or Secretary Seddon, right up to the President himself. Since all records are missing, accurate knowledge is impossible. No wonder historians rarely touch on the planning behind the Northern Campaign.

Be that as it may, there was a Cabinet member immensely irritated: Postmaster General John Reagan. The others were disturbed enough to show up—*uninvited, impromptu, and without prior knowledge of the others*—at the President's home on Sunday afternoon, 17 May, to find out what was going on. The Postmaster General was among them. There was confabulation of some sort; no one knew for sure what was going on.

Second thoughts … even thirds … about Lee's plan emerged in those chanced meetings. Mystified sharp intellects in the Cabinet and run-of-the-mill thinkers similarly were confused. Unsettled to a man, the whole cabinet showed up on Sunday at different times. Southern leadership was floundering while the war was at a decisive moment.

In all probability Lee was perceived either as intellectually dangerous with such an unusual plan or else in manifest danger of being destroyed by the Federal army. The rising anxiety among the Cabinet members was so tangible they felt compelled to impinge upon President Davis.

Reputedly the plan had been approved with Lee present sometime during the previous three days, but on the fourth day they felt compelled to go to the President for comprehension, without Lee present. Cabinet members wanted an "objective" interpretation of the plan, as if they would, or could, get one from their president.

Apparently they thought President Davis knew what was intrinsic to the plan; in consequence they interjected themselves into his private life. Lee was already heading back to his military headquarters so he knew nothing of the depth of their puzzlement nor the width of their grievances. The Confederate Cabinet's disquiet was so strong that President Davis scheduled another meeting to mull over the matter; an extra meeting that might well view the plan with a jaundiced eye.

Something big was up in Southern military matters, no doubt about it, in May 1863. It was bigger than their previously attempted invasion of the North that ended in defeat at Sharpsburg/Antietam, Maryland in September of 1862. Why try again? Was Lee's different approach this time workable? Was it necessary?

No way exists for us to determine whether or not R. E. Lee told the full extent of his purpose and plan, specifically since other officials— with numerous ears and almost as many tongues—were involved in the planning sessions. But Lee knew something that they didn't.

One can only presume Lee operated per usual—silence, secrecy, *in pectore*, silent heart. He played it close to his vest; discreet about details, understated, with hushed or muted emphases and implications. That secretiveness was the same nature as his famous compatriot's, General Thomas "Stonewall" Jackson. Both knew well that one should "speak only to improve upon the silence," and did so in military matters to the consternation of subordinates, or outsiders not privy to military ways.

Most people realize how difficult it is to change personal patterns of communication. When one is "the" authority, in command or in modern parlance "has the microphone," the center of attention and action, how can give-and-take occur? How can information and dialogue really take place in such environments?

So if the mode of authoritarianism worked ... or appeared to work ... why then change the pattern of communication?

Add to that assumption the deeper one that we human beings love our own idiosyncrasies, our eccentricities, so well so that we think we need *not* change them. The result is we use them over and over. Re-use reinforces our self-approval rating, promptly demonstrating to ourselves we're lovable, right, and virtuous—just plain wonderful! For adults, even the best among us, that self-approval is nothing more than juvenile "self-pleasuring," so gratifying to so many. And not only boys.

Accordingly, it's not unreasonable to embrace an understanding that the mature Robert Lee reverted to his usual technique of quiet command at the best, or secrecy at the worst.

There isn't evidence that he told the whole purpose and/or plan with all facets and subtleties noted. Pencil-pushing, managerial, officialized executives could have been pushed into dismay at Lee's usual minimal presentations. They could have slipped into a simplistic mindset: accepting easy answers to difficult questions.

Whatever the case, Davis' Cabinet members were awfully disturbed. They wanted to hear more on their individual and official terms from the commander who was accustomed to making sweeping, mammoth life-and-death decisions. They wanted to deal with necessary matters from technical and departmental perspectives, which might or might not be vetoed by President Davis.

Lee, on the other hand, fashioned battlefields where hundreds and thousands of men had to fight to stay alive in varying locales where killing and ruination would take place, sometimes on his terms, but often as not, on the enemy's. Contrasted with his concerns, theirs may well have been minuscule to Lee. So the gentleman general applied his minimalist approach of playing everything close to his vest *as per usual.*

It is wearisome to any serious searcher for the truth about the South's Northern Campaign of 1863 to find what R. E. Lee actually presented to the Richmond authorities. What specific action—or non-action—was intended by the highly intelligent General Commanding is a mystery.

But we can grasp it implicitly: deception is the core of military strategy. Military soulmate, General Thomas "Stonewall" Jackson, insisted the first rule of successful warfare is: *"Always mystify, mislead, and surprise your enemy."* Lee agreed.

Mystify. Mislead. Surprise. Lee would do all three to his enemies—and to his own side, first! Yes, by all appearances he applied mystification unhesitatingly to top Confederate authorities and later to top officers of the Northern Campaign.

One can imagine the icy reaction he would have received had he candidly informed the Cabinet members that he *"did not intend a general battle"* across the Mason-Dixon Line. Or how intolerable it would have sounded to his generals that he "did not intend a general battle *unless attacked"* while in the North? On either level some would have thought him utterly egotistical because of his military ingenuity; others would have considered him in no way fit to lead an army. It's possible some one might have exclaimed, "Whose side are you on?" Which question may have been on John Reagan's mind.

Wouldn't someone at the meetings, maybe Adjutant General Cooper, have asked a prior question? "As a military master, have you had enough time to think through your proposal in the two weeks since your battle at Chancellorsville?"

If it were the case that he would win a military victory up North of any sort—as great as Chancellorsville, or greater—it eventually would look incredulous to friend and foe alike. In the best series of development he couldn't possibly stay northward to garner the fruits of his labor.

Northern generals had stayed in the South though defeated, but they didn't play the role of conquered enemy. Lee's movements even after victory would be back to Virginia, out of the North, looking trounced in retrograde. Had it not registered on him that he would have to return to Southern soil? Wouldn't that movement look to all as a repeat of the previous year's retreat from Sharpsburg/Antietam in Maryland?

But there is deepest question. Was Robert Lee planning an all-out battle to win the war in one massive, overwhelming battle, as various "experts" contend that he intended his invasion to accomplish? And, if so, why was President Davis—who finally agreed to the plan—so parsimonious in transferring troops to his command, especially those divisions stationed along the southern seaboard?

Of equal import, in such a war-winning battle that "experts" think he intended, likely there would have been high-rate losses similar to those suffered at Chancellorsville. Or losses even higher, on the enemy's home soil—as actually happened, the still higher rates at Gettysburg. Such a "war-ending" battle would have been a Pyrrhic victory of monumental proportions that again the South could not afford. In name, an all-out, knock-'em-dead battle is impressive; in reality it would have been lethal to the Southern cause.

If Robert E. Lee had laid out the peculiar particulars completely, giving details of his plan over those four days in May, most likely the planners would not have consented to the invasion. Participants obviously detected some sort of weakness in what he did present. Chances are the ramifications were too imprecise to satisfy fretful minds.

It is not unreasonable to assume Lee may never have mentioned unintended consequences. Bare sketches rather than itemized details likely were shared with politicians, who, after all, are simply ordinary people with portfolios. Lee's reserved presentation might have had both a "good" reason and the "real" reason: loose lips lose battles.

Plausibly he told them somewhat of common military matters, mentioning states and generals involved, which units and what numbers, timelines and equipment, maybe even areas to be traveled to get where he was going. Estimates of what enemy units would be encountered and appraisal of their military capabilities surely would have regaled civilian officials.

R. E. Lee, Southern landowner, absolutely would have told them of the teeming agricultural spoils that would result from his venture into the rich farmland of southcentral Pennsylvania. Particularly he would have reminded them that the area was peopled by pacifists: Pennsylvania Dutchmen of Amish, Brethren, Mennonite, and Quaker religious persuasions. All such peripheral considerations would have made favorable impressions. At first, anyway.

Afterwards, serious second assessments would have occurred because each Cabinet member must have conceded—at least to himself—that peripheral conditions were a smokescreen of sorts. Or, if they did consent to Lee's purpose and plan in the meetings, they could have been making serious reassessments while he was speaking.

The true reason for not clarifying the probabilities inherent in the Northern Campaign presumably was that Lee understood there were imponderables. He had but a few weeks to plan an invasion with all its concomitant issues after the victory at Chancellorsville. How many new issues there would be, the military master couldn't know.

Nor did R. E. Lee have anyone with whom he could discuss details: "Stonewall" was dead. Lee's military equal, Jackson, had been wounded at Chancellorsville from shots fired at eventide by his own men thinking he was a Northern cavalryman. He had an arm amputated, and subsequently was felled by pneumonia after the victory. Lee sent a message to Jackson, before his death, about Jackson's inestimable worth: "You have lost your left arm but I my right!" All too true! Lee lost other appendages—at Gettysburg.

He needed Jackson for the Pennsylvania Campaign, to plan, and, if necessary, to fight. But Lee's mighty right arm was gone. He was effectively alone in President Davis' office, though there were people around him: old Adjutant General Cooper, tight-faced Secretary of War Seddon, neuralgic-faced President Davis. And, the five Cabinet members doing their patriotic duties were not strategists.

The best possibility for someone to fill Jackson's place was Jefferson Davis, Lee's former West Point peer, and that wasn't feasible politically, militarily—or temperamentally. However, Davis was seriously ill. He wasn't even capable of accepting Lee's invitation to visit army headquarters. Busy with administrative duties, the President had to struggle somberly with poor health, and, oppressively, with the recalcitrant Confederate Congress, although they mutually detested one another. He was in no condition for anything, *anything*, but not military action at all.

For President Davis there was a miserable appendage to being Chief Executive. It was so deleterious to him because it escalated his physical maladies more than most people knew until after the war. The next-room war clerk noted in a similar situation that, "The President is at work at his residence, not yet come down to the office; and I learn it is difficult to get his attention to any business just now but *appointments*. ... No doubt he is anxious and very unhappy."[2]

Davis had to study and answer the incessant—and shameful—requests by the daily dozens for military advancements. So many well-to-do planters did not want to serve in the army yet wanted to be Southern colonels. It was pathetic! Southern gentry were sure they were all officer material. The lowest form of patriots seeking the highest offices as they walked the city streets of Richmond—earning Lee's disparagement, too, but usually in letters to family members and seldom, if ever, expressed publicly.

There wasn't a replacement for Stonewall. Lee knew it. Everyone knew it.

However, odds on Lee's psychological strategy carried the day. Assessments at night by the Cabinet participants were another story. Nothing satisfied them enough, either individually or as a body, about the General's venture. Business about the Summer Campaign was unfinished, four days planning in May 1863 notwithstanding.

The extemporaneous Sunday appearances by the individual Cabinet members on 17 May at President Davis' residence became an absolute necessity.

Uncertainty was rife in the Confederate executive branch of government about the next military move. Doubt raised suspicion of the leading general's purpose and plan.

In contrast, Robert Edward Lee was riding to his headquarters with keen dedication to his purpose, eager to get the Army of Northern Virginia on the road. He was going northward with a scheme; going to a place few knew anything about.

If he had mentioned the uncertainty of his Northern Campaign to Confederate officialdom they would have been very concerned—and rightly so.

If he had not mentioned the uncertainty to Confederate officialdom they would have been very concerned—and rightly so, to the nth degree.

R. E. Lee was pressured by quandary after quandary though he had won victory after victory. Not a fake army but the Army of the Potomac stared at him across woodlands, fields, and rivers—mornings, noons and nights.

A huge emotional bulldog—those victories that did not attain Victory—tracked General Robert Edward Lee. Ceaselessly.

Chapter Notes

1. Ethan Sepp Rafuse. Robert E. Lee and The Fall off the Confederacy, 1863-1865 (Lanham, MD: Rowan and Littlefield, 2009): 37.
2. J. B. Jones. A Rebel War Clerk's Diary. II. 362.

CHAPTER 16

"Everything Was Risky"

LEE'S PLAN WAS as well conceived as possible—but not as a military operation.

It was a psychological procedure posing as a military operation: *rara avis*. Strange indeed. Military operations and psychological procedures are different species, not just two sides of the same coin. They could work out well together, cross-fertilizing one another, but that's a bird more rare. Given that distinction, Lee's army would do its duty militarily if the psychological procedure came under attack by Federal forces, he'd see to that occurrence.

The possibility of attack on Lee's army by Federal forces made for problems, uncommonly instanced by his purposely severed supply line. That rash act weighed down on the Army of Northern Virginia, along with its physical gear, tents, guns, ammunition, provender and cannons. The ANV's heaviest burden was the emotional weight of psychological warfare's arguable validity and dubious effectiveness.

The real problem is that psychological warriors get ahead of themselves, so to speak. They think that thought/idea/theory, itself, trumps concrete/empirical action. They tend to reason that analysis, itself, solves problems. Just because thinking, for the most part, precedes action doesn't mean it's correct. Psychological warriors tend to bite off over-sized chunks of intellectual elements that they nibble or gnaw at, endeavors gaining limited sustenance.

Present-day military theory calls it "a bridge-too-far." Psychological warriors "see" much—and miss much, too. They assure themselves that they've covered all possibilities, that they don't *necessarily* need to have *bona fide* tangible, on-the-spot experiences before they plan their next move. Yet simulations are not facts-on-the-ground that can verify nooks and crannies, hidden places and distinct possibilities, sounds and even odors that bespeak an enemy's presence. And intangibles, because untouchable, even ghostly, cannot be factored into plans. But they damned well exist!

In short, the psychologizing of motive, or event, or "condition-on-the-ground" might be close to reality, but 'tis not reality. It is not concrete. It's fantasizing eleven inches short of a foot. Everything is illusory, virtual. "Virtual" programs and games are not so much bad as trivial, piddling attempts at the genuine world. Of course, when there is a real, live, wartime enemy who wants to kill, suicide-bomb or nuke persons, then psychologizing about that enemy and enemy actions is treacherous, an IED lurking, heavy, swarming with consequences both intended and unintended.

Why treacherous, dangerous, risky? In the main, because the enemy is doing the same as the psychological warrior. Turn-about-is-fair-action twists everything out of position and no one knows concretely which way is up, what is actual. The situation is distorted perilously and may fail precipitously on a trifle.

Doubtless then, both sides can fake themselves out of position because they don't apprehend the true situation of the other side, seeing the other side through a distorting lens. In fact, the risk of failure is optimized for both, sometimes ending in a "lose/lose" situation rather than a "win/lose"—but never a "win/win." Non-understanding or mishaps are distinct possibilities in psychological warfare attacks, *a la* Pearl Harbor: the Japanese didn't know how massive the American response would be.

Mayhem is the worst possibility of faking oneself out of position in psychological warfare, *a la* nuclear attacks at Hiroshima and Nagasaki. The Japanese never calculated their mishap at Pearl Harbor would result in double-mushroom cloud-whammies to end their non-understanding into obliteration by the erasure of two cities.

R. E. Lee's plan for proclaiming peace up north at a special place was psychological. He may not have seen the inherent fragility of such an approach. With the plan in his sights as a noble venture for peace he didn't—possibly, couldn't—have his enemy in comprehensible sight. Certainly it was not in visible sight as he headed east from Chambersburg to his intended site beyond Gettysburg. People interested in the Northern Campaign know he didn't know where the Union army was. His vision was so blurred that he couldn't determine it was actually in the field anywhere, except where he *wanted* it to be: around Washington, D.C. People in the know in the Confederacy also thought the Federal Army of the Potomac would be there. "Precisely at this time [14 June 1863] the enemy disappeared from Fredericksburg seemingly designing to cover Washington."[1]

In truth, while practicing psychological warfare a leader has to have veritable double vision: heuristic evidence of the enemy's deceptive practices *and* empirical evidence of his military operations. Both evidences need be irrefutable. Robert Lee didn't have a single clue that was "clear and distinct," as Descartes would say, about either of those conditions. His men were marching into never-never land, and never knew it. It wasn't the Old Dominion they were in. There was a new Devil's Den waiting.

General Lee unequivocally had to consider that the commander of the Northern army was perpetrating deception of some sort on him. He had no such evidence.

General Lee unequivocally had to consider that the enemy commander was up to no tricks but was in a mode and a mood to fight. He had no such evidence.

Lee was heading for failure in a picturesque place, a big time failure.

Psychological warfare is risky. It's much like a liar lying to another liar. Which liar gains what? Which liar knows who has an advantage or not? How does a liar find the truth about the other liar in such a situation?

Lee had little, if any, reason to act. He didn't know much of what was happening back in Virginia, in Maryland along his way, in Washington, nor manifestly within Pennsylvania, where he was headed.

What he did have was belief in a cause. Men died for his belief in his plan. Yet more than men died: his great belief in his men was circumscribed because he asked too much of them, causing many *good* men to die. His over-belief in his hastily crafted plan and his faulty belief that the Federal army would be back guarding Washington began the catastrophe that took another two years to materialize at Appomattox Court House.

Possibly, not probably, each or both of Lee's beliefs were true and good—but belief is not enough. He forgot that the other side also had beliefs. Did he so much as consider theirs might be truer and better? He apparently forgot that it must be the right truth, the right good, that alone is worthy of belief. The right truth and the right goodness are not determined by one's upbringing, or culture, or indoctrination. Or by wishes; even if sincere, they're still nothing but wishes.

R. E. Lee found the circumstances in Pennsylvania to be highly dangerous. The gravity of the danger was not simply that he was on enemy soil in the soft underbelly of the North but that the enemy was, for practical purposes, invisible. Invisibility is the greatest deception imaginable for a warrior. Where invisibility reigns, any possible thing can happen. What the warrior believes in such a circumstance has very little to do with what will happen to him, or to his opponent.

"Everything was risky in our war. I knew often that I was playing a very bold game but it was the only *possible* one."[2] Famous words, but the truth of Lee's conclusion is a question. *What happens when bold risks become the only possible game?* And the answer to that question is a terrifying one: defeat. Defeat came with deaths by the thousands, followed by excuses, allegations, and recriminations by the hundreds of thousands during the remainder of the war—and for 150 years since.

He should have listened to many a mother's assertion: "When in doubt, don't!"

R. E. Lee's game was over-believed in. And overly psychologized. So many died needlessly, away from home. On enemy soil. The South's death gurgle began up North.

Lee lived on.

Lee lived on ... to regret it?

To forget it?

To pay for it.

Chapter Notes

1. John B. Jones. A Rebel War Clerk's Diary at the Confederate States Capital. (Phila.: Lippincott, 1866): Vol. II. 12.
2. William Allen, "Memoranda of Conversations With Lee" in Gary Gallagher, Ed. Lee The Soldier. Lincoln: Univ. of Nebraska Press, 1996, 17.

CHAPTER 17

Needed: A "Fake" Army

THE FEDERAL ARMY would fall back or be called back around Washington, D. C. whenever a Southern army would get close. Robert Lee knew that fact full well in 1861 and '62.

Lee had written to Jefferson Davis of the "great exertions for the safety of Washington," as the core of Northern military policy in the Eastern Theater of operations. He was positive that, "The well known anxiety of the Northern Government for the safety of its capital would induce it to *retain* a large force for its defense and thus sensibly *relieve* the opposition to our advance" northward.[1] That Northern defensive move would work to his advantage, he reasoned.

Abraham Lincoln had been resolute: the center of the Federal government and resistance to the Rebels should be free "from the rockets red glare, the bombs bursting in air" to give "proof that our flag was still there" to the Northern populace. Lee knew that fact just as well. It was sure to work to his advantage, he reasoned.

The rationale is patently obvious. The District of Columbia bordered a slave state, Virginia, while at the same time was surrounded on three sides by Maryland. The Chesapeake Bay State was a slave state, kept within the Union by what was nominally a military occupation. Its large city of Baltimore was decidedly pro-Southern, pro-slavery, pro-Secessionist, and pro-Rebellion. They were Rebel wolves in Union wool.

From time to time Baltimore was named—superficially—Charm

City. Actually it was a seething pot, about ready in 1863 to boil over and scald the Lincoln government. If mutiny happened in Bal-more, as locals pronounced it, the nation's capital would have been critically menaced.

Only ten or eleven leagues southward, Washington was a steady nine hours or more on horseback, with the possibility of wagons and buggies alongside. Guns and ammunition, and maybe secreted cannon, limber and caisson would add another three or four hours travel time. By any calculation, Baltimore was near enough to Washington to cause consternation and fear in Washington.

Had President Davis been physically able to accept the General's invitation in May to visit the site of the Chancellorsville victory, one of the "many things" Lee would have sought to discuss would have been his plan to invade Pennsylvania. He would want to mystify the Federal army. His plan would make it appear not to threaten Washington by maneuvering westward as his army traveled toward Harpers Ferry, then northward through Maryland—where he had lost a bloody battle in 1862. Continuing into Pennsylvania, he could then give assent to Northern fears that he might circumnavigate Washington and attack it from the north, or, conceivably, from the east. Whether from north or east, Washington's defensive postures were suspect.

It turned out that Lee's maneuvering gave sufficient appearance—temporarily—that the West was his target and he would not be heading northeast to D.C. In fact, that suspicion had a loud ring of truth about it. As late as 17 June 1863 Joseph Hooker, then Commanding General of the Northern Army of the Potomac, actually suggested to the Union General-in-Chief Henry Halleck that Lee might be moving troops to the West.[2] Maybe to Vicksburg! It was a reasonable assumption; the besieged Confederate stronghold on the Mississippi River was in dire need of help because General Ulysses Grant was laying waste to Vicksburg with battering assaults.

Robert Lee had his plan on the right track. His assumption was every inch realistic; he would mystify, mislead, and surprise the enemy. As late as 21 June he noted in correspondence with President

Davis "the Federal Army was apparently guarding the approaches to Washington and manifested no disposition to assume the offensive."[3]

Having expressed that point, Lee still would have needed to know one other fact, the primary fact: Was the Union Army of the Potomac following his army?

All his maneuvering gave the appearance that if Lee's army was not moving to the West, he still was not heading towards Washington. The imagined circumnavigation to the north or east of D. C. gave the impression he was not after the enemy's capital. Nonetheless it remained imaginable that he just might circumnavigate westward, then north, then head east in order to pounce upon the Northern Capital from either the north or the east.

The wise General knew he needed space free of military competition to perform his special act. And mystification works wonders—easily on the theatrical stage, but on the military stage almost as easily. He wanted his opponents fixed territorially on Washington, not only fixated emotionally.

General Lee sized up the geography well. He knew there wasn't anything of military importance that would necessitate protection by the Northern army in Pennsylvania's southern tier, from west to east, of Franklin, Adams, and York counties. The towns of Chambersburg, Gettysburg, and York were located centrally in each county respectively, and were clearly accessible. No Federal military presence at all. The area was home to docile pacifist Pennsylvania Dutchmen, beautiful countrysides, rich farmlands, small populations, and nary a Yankee Bluecoat. This piece of Pennsylvania seemed made to raid for supplies. It was an even greater place to accomplish a peace proposal. Perhaps only New York City would have been a better target, but it was 200 miles farther away, and too big to handle.

Lee saw that the three-county area was utilizable, like in-season fruit—ripe, plentiful, free for the picking. Any *perceptive* architect of peace could see the locale as an available prize with minimal expenditure of resources; "by maneuvering merely," as Jefferson Davis wrote. It was part of a psychological approach that would catch the enemy by surprise, so that "a most important result would be cheaply attained," as Davis also noted.

A sizable portion of R. E. Lee's reasoning would include the awareness that he needed time to engineer and perfect the psychological warfare angle: proclamation of peace to the inhabitants of the North on their soil. Lee reasoned and used a superior propaganda effort: *not* engaging in combat.

Too, pillaging was strictly forbidden by order of General Lee. Southerners had maintained that Northern troops were thieves and destroyers of property when invading Dixieland. R. E. Lee didn't want to induce fear in the Northern populace so he gave strict orders *not* to destroy property *nor* violate civilians in any manner. Also, they were to pay for any thing commandeered. Pay with Southern scrip, that is. It was "provisional money" that would be useable if, and, only if, the Southern cause were successful.

Despite the novelty and specifics of his grand scheme, Lee necessarily needed to have a big-time action, muscular and brash. Showy. He needed something to assure that the huge Army of the Potomac would actually fall back to protect Washington. He didn't want to leave such an important matter to chance.

Fearing its Capital would be captured again and burned as the British had done fifty years before, during the War of 1812—capitol building, executive mansion, government buildings, devastated—the North was thoroughly ill at ease so close to Rebeldom. The action Lee wanted performed would have to be a clear distraction that would freeze the Northern army in place around D. C., a substantial distance—say 100 miles—from his own self-determined place for a peace proposal.

To that end R. E. Lee devised a plan. Wisdom dictated the necessity of another Confederate army, of some sort, to pin down the Federal Army of the Potomac. That second army would be so stationed in northeastern Virginia to appear as an offensive force fronting the Northern capital. Such action would cause the Federals to bolt back to the Potomac River, dutifully preserving Abe Lincoln's government and reputation. Deception is always at the heart of strategy, so that plan would likely succeed.

Robert E. Lee formalized his strategy in correspondence with President Davis in what can only be perceived as a precious particle of truth, a gem of historical truth come down to us to interpret and use:

> If an army could be organized under the command of General Beauregard and pushed forward to Culpepper Court-House, *threatening Washington* from that direction, it would not only effect diversion most favorable for this army, but would, I think, relieve us of any apprehension of an attack upon Richmond during our absence. The well known anxiety of the Federal Government for the safety of its capital would induce it to retain a large force for its defense, and thus sensibly *relieve the opposition* to our advance. … I think it most important that whatever troops be used for the purpose I named, General Beauregard be placed in command … His presence would give *magnitude* to even a small demonstration, and tend greatly *to perplex and confound the enemy.*[4]

> … If the plan I suggested the other day, of organizing an army, *an army in effigy,* and General Beauregard at Culpepper Court-House, can be carried into effect, *much relief* can be afforded.[5]

One has but to recall a similar incident in World War II to realize the positive efficacy of General Lee's recommendation for a sham army, "an army in effigy." In 1944 Supreme Allied Commander General Dwight Eisenhower chose a leader for a similar Army: General George Patton. If any general had "magnitude" it was he. Patton commanded, in high style and with publicity well placed to reach the Nazi Germans, a dummy army in southeast England opposite Calais, France. Eisenhower's plan was to compel the enemy to think that the cross-English Channel invasion of "Fortress Europe" in *Operation Overlord* would take place at that narrow passage rather than any other place along the Channel. Dictator Adolph Hitler was sucked in by Eisenhower's deception. *Der Führer* believed the stratagem and misplaced his prized Panzer tank divisions in the Calais area, away from the real invasion point on the beaches of Normandy, France, in June 1944.

Back in 1863, Confederate Commander-in-Chief Jefferson Davis rejected his General's recommendation for a dummy army. Davis's military perception didn't accept the reasoning behind the plan to threaten the enemy's capital, even though a high-profile Confederate general was supposed to lead "the army in effigy."

Confederate General Lee accepted his chief's rejection, and obeyed, resulting in disaster. The enemy found Lee; there wasn't an "army in effigy" fronting Washington to freeze them in place.

With no sham army as a ruse, the Union army had no need to fall back to protect Washington. The Union troops were supremely directed by Union Commander-in-Chief Abraham Lincoln. It was he who told the commander of the Army of the Potomac crisply, "Lee's army is your objective."[6] Federal Generals Hooker and Meade obeyed their chief's order. Those leaders had an army that followed them— and Abraham Lincoln.

Lee was found. Lee was fought. Lee was defeated.

The Southern invasion of the North—no matter how courageously its army fought at Gettysburg—was ended. And the bloodiest battle ever fought in the Western Hemisphere was a defeat for the Confederacy, starting its downward spiral, corkscrewing its way towards Hell.

Confederate victories at Fredericksburg and Chancellorsville fundamentally meant nothing for they did not result in the peace that General Lee wanted to proclaim. Both those courageous victories, therefore, ended as meaningless to the Southern cause. They became military textbook material. Winning quickly can be turned into losing.

Two years later peace happened.

If only the Federal Army had fallen back to protect Washington, D.C. Robert E. Lee would have had peace happen his way, in his place.

Lee had noted smartly the historical value of a certain locale from America's founding years. That place possessed something the *confederation* of Southern states would note as a trophy of immediate political worth. The degree of importance would never be determined because the battle at Gettysburg interfered. The South would have immediately gotten the implication and ramification of the locale Lee wanted to use as a platform for the proposal of peace. On the other side, Northerners would have gained an education in history, albeit a cramming, as slow learners usually have to take their medicine.

Chapter Notes

1. WR/OR. I. 27. 3. 924f (Emphasis added)
2. WR/OR. I. 27. 1. 50.
3. Ibid. 315.
4. WR/OR. I. 27. 3. 925. (Emphases added)
5. Ibid. 931. (Emphasis added)
6. Abraham Lincoln in communiqué to General Joseph Hooker on 10 June 1863 at 6:40 PM. See: WR/OR/. I/ 27. 1. 35.

CHAPTER 18

The Soft Underbelly

THE THREE SOUTHCENTRAL Pennsylvania counties R. E. Lee intended to envelope and take control of were devoid of Northern defenses and could be surprised, and seized handily.

Franklin, Adams, and York Counties were exposed. After Lee's previous thrust northward in September 1862, which ended at Sharpsburg, Maryland, the Lincoln Administration had not instituted any defensive protections in the soft underbelly of the North. The area was an open invitation to Southern incursions.

A Federal army depot and a medical center at Chambersburg, nine months earlier, had served as a hospital for wounded soldiers from that Confederate defeat at Sharpsburg/Antietem. So there was something military—in the loosest application of the term—located in Franklin County, the westernmost of the three counties. There also was a military hospital in York County. Neither a medical center nor a hospital could be considered operationally military, that is, a defense against invaders of the three counties. The Northern underbelly was a beautiful act of Nature, but it was squishy militarily.

So it was that General Jeb Stuart, the South's jaunty cavalryman, only a month *after* the 1862 Confederate defeat in Maryland, rode past the Sharpsburg battlefield area with 1,800 cavalry troopers as a slap in the face to the "victors" of Antietam. Heading north into Pennsylvania for Chambersburg, in Franklin County, the Confederates captured it with ease, to the distress of the local citizenry. The Lincoln

Administration gave the Rebel raid slight notice—and no protection. So much for preserving the Union!

In Chambersburg Stuart "appropriated" hundreds of horses, destroyed railroad property leading west to Pittsburgh, and "captured" eight black men and boys to take back to Virginia.

For all we know Stuart did a job on Chambersburg simply because abolitionist John Brown had established a staging area there for his cohorts and supplies from June to October 1859. Chambersburg, Pennsylvania was one of two locales where Brown prepared for his Harpers Ferry, Virginia raid on the Federal arsenal. John Brown had wanted to start a slave revolt, so Stuart surmised Chambersburg needed to be punished for harboring his efforts. Haters of John Brown thought that way, even long after his failed raid, capture and hanging.

Robert Lee had been in charge of the 1859 operation to retake the Federal arsenal, commanding Jeb Stuart and U.S. Marines. But the real action had occurred at Harpers Ferry before the Marines arrived. "Captain John Sinn, of the Frederick, Maryland militia, arrived on Monday evening [17 October 1859] 'Every man [there] had a gun, and four-fifths under no command,' he reported."[1] Local militia and armed citizens had put the Federal property under siege, confining the abolitionists by outgunning, outshooting, and corralling them. The insurrectionists were surrounded, holed up with no practical means of escape.

The Marines arrived *after* the major action was concluded and had but to mop up; they did so in record time. Colonel Lee wrote in his official report, "The whole thing was over in a few minutes." Five, to be exact! The local militias in Virginia and Maryland with the armed civilians had "captured" the insurgents. Robert E. Lee was acclaimed the hero. Fame, like God, moves in a mysterious way.

As an historical bauble it can be noted that Robert Lee was returned to Harpers Ferry by order of President James Buchanan at the time of John Brown's hanging in late 1859. Lee was commander of the artillery in case some attempt was made to rescue Brown. Nothing much happened, except Brown and his men—white men who fought to free black men—became martyrs in the developing crusade against slavery while under Robert E. Lee's guardianship; in one of history's many ironies. John Brown became immortal in song and legend.

Jeb Stuart remembered that 1859 action well. Later Chambersburg suffered in the invasion of 1863. Revenge takes bizarre forms.

Colorful as he was, Stuart made invasion of the North seem easy. Even after Lee's failed attempt at Antietam in September 1862, Federal precautions to prevent incursions had not been taken by the year 1863. The southern tier counties of Pennsylvania were "easy pickin's" as the squishy underbelly of the North.

It should be noted further, as an additional demonstration of the lackadaisical attitude of the North to protect itself, that the year *after* its bitter defeat at Gettysburg the South *again* invaded the North and sacked Chambersburg! The town was burned down almost completely in July 1864—to the utter distress of its inhabitants. Where was Lincoln?

That 1864 mini-invasion was the third of three such shameful events. The Lincoln Administration gave the-year-after-Gettysburg event slight notice. Where was Lincoln, indeed? Heads should have rolled. So intent was that Administration on invading the South that it took almost no precautions about the North being invaded various times. So much for protection and preservation of the Union!

Many Northerners considered the situation a dereliction of responsibility. Did no one care in Washington? Did military officials think that the independence-seeking Rebels wouldn't want to broaden the war beyond their own borders?

Blatantly, the Union was negligent about its soil—except the District of Columbia. Did anyone in official Washington note that Pennsylvania is a mere 20 to 30 miles from Virginia through the narrowest north-south area of Maryland? There was a reason the Southern invasions followed such a route.

That proximity made the squishy underbelly of the North in southcentral Pennsylvania provocatively inviting. It kept tempting Lee. Several times "Stonewall" Jackson had called for an invasion there. He realized someone in Washington was asleep at the switch.

In late Spring 1863 the Army of Northern Virginia Commander sized up the situation with a sharp eye, keen intellect, will to win, and a plan as buoyant and phenomenal as anything Jeb Stuart could do.

But why would Lee attempt to go there again? He had been halted in Maryland in the bloodiest day of the war, on the way northward, only nine months before in September 1862. Hadn't he learned his lesson? What *military* results, acclaim, or victory could be attained with no Union army present in those counties to defeat, since, by his reasoning, the Union Army of the Potomac would be back defending Washington, D.C.?

Did R. E. Lee have something else, a Jackson-maneuver of some misleading, mystifying, and surprising sort to accomplish in the summer of '63? Was there a "bigger fish to fry" that would negate the few nagging misgivings about a repeat attempt to reach Northern soil?

"Lee could not afford many more battles like Chancellorsville which later he claimed left him *'more depressed than after Fredericksburg'* because his army *'had prevailed at a cost that nearly cancelled out whatever tactical and operational benefits had been gained.'*"[2] Since he couldn't afford this kind of victory again, Lee needed a new kind, a *different* sort of victory. He needed a victory that would be truly victorious: peace.

Doubtless, he was seeking victory, however *not* an all-out, aggressive, unrestrained combat-driven conquest. His report had stated unequivocally, "*it had not been intended to fight a general battle … unless attacked.*" The operative phrase was *not intended to fight.* A victory was still intended or he wouldn't have been up north with 65,000-70,000 loyal troops.

Some thought—and others still think the same thing today—Lee planned a military victory on a battlefield against a much larger army. He had done it two months prior. They expected a gigantic brawl like Fredericksburg and/or a surgical operation like Chancellorsville that would decisively:

1) defeat the much larger Federal army at a site in its own territory, Pennsylvania, which simultaneously would interfere with and influence Federal forces throughout the whole Confederacy by causing them to sue for peace, also *somehow* relieving the siege at Vicksburg, Mississippi nearly a thousand miles away; or

2) ruin Abraham Lincoln and remove him from the American political scene because he was perpetuating the war;

3) cause Abolitionists to "beat their swords into plowshares" and Radical Republicans "their spears into pruning hooks." Chroniclers often think huge thoughts—after events.

Such wrong-headed thoughts about Lee's purpose—*contra* Lee's decidedly clear statement that he *did not intend a general battle, unless attacked*—would be a "Miracle of Miracles" and would solve all the South's problems. Realistically, it is an *Argumentum ad ignorantiam!*

We need to remember that Lee told his son, Custis, only a "revolution" against Lincoln's administration by the Union populace would stop the war.[3]

For that reason we can fathom that General Lee was set to provide a basis for the revolution: a psychological basis.

It would be a campaign with the usual *military* planning and execution serving as protection for his true plan in a Northern state so he could "*proclaim* ... PEACE to the inhabitants," without destruction of civilians or their property, as Lee's General Order 73 explicitly stated.

Such a campaign would excite Northerners from Maine to Maryland, Maryland to Missouri, Missouri to Minnesota, Minnesota back to Maine again—and every state inside that perimeter—to petition for peace. A peace on honorable terms.

So it was that Lee's attempt to spark a revolution up north began with an expedition into the soft underbelly of the North.

Lieutenant General Richard Ewell's Second Corps—"Stonewall" Jackson's old corps—marched into Pennsylvania's Franklin County. Lee then did what he had done before: divide his army. He divided and subdivided it. Several times! Jeb Stuart's cavalry division was split, some going to Pennsylvania, some remaining in Virginia. Two-thirds of Ewell's Corps was sent 55 miles northeast of Chambersburg towards Harrisburg, the other third 60 miles due east to York, to position them along the Susquehanna River, 30 miles apart. Lee then would have two corps left. To fight a general battle with his units dispersed over 2,800 square miles? One must think again.

That river supplied the largest amount of water to the Chesapeake Bay, moistening Tidewater, Virginia then flowing to the Atlantic Ocean. It had been Confederate yearning—and at some point military planning—to go to the "banks of the Susquehanna."

The Susquehanna River held an abstract attraction; one could say a value, for Confederate leaders. They didn't speak of going to the banks of the Schuylkill, flowing through Philadelphia—the main manufacturing center for the North throughout the war. Nor did they speak of going to the banks of the Hudson, flowing by New York—the main shipping hub and immigration center for the North throughout the war.

"The banks of the Susquehanna" had special meaning for Southerners, for all one knows, a fixation. Perhaps the reason was that a bit farther west of those banks the American government had taken refuge during the Revolutionary War, beyond the reach of the British Army. Then again perhaps it was that geologically the area appeared to be a northern extension of the Shenandoah Valley's fertile rolling landscape. A more understandable scenario is that the river had political significance: a barrier that had to be crossed.

The Susquehanna was a borderline. It was a wavy-lined diagonal border from northwest to southeast between agricultural pursuits southward and industries to the east.

To the south was an agrarian economy stretching northward through the Valley of western Virginia, in and straightaway out of Maryland, into southcentral Pennsylvania and then eastward to the river. To the east beyond that river borderline lay the more industrialized areas, the cities of the North with their larger populations, although some agriculture was successful in the area east of that borderline.

Overall, the Susquehanna was a psychological margin, not an imaginary one but a concrete line that was at the same time fluid. It was a line flowing between the sylvan world of former times and the modernity of the mid-nineteenth century's Industrial Revolution.

Psychological borders are powerful motivators. They are serious human realities, dynamic in nature and effective in operation. General Robert E. Lee, militarily, wanted to secure a border; the physical and psychological borderline of the Susquehanna River. For a psychological purpose.

There was a prevalent fable that he was going to run roughshod over Pennsylvania, as far east as Philadelphia. Without a supply line? Get real!

Publics North and South, like most peoples, loved fables. Some of Lee's general officers made up fables, like capturing Philadelphia, while enduring silence and secrecy from their Commander. Fabulating around a campfire is big-time recreation. R. E. Lee maintained silence. Fables grew in number, with wishful thinking.

In Lee's discerning eyes movement so far through Pennsylvania would be an improbability without a supply line. Yet various extremists up North imagined, flightily, that he would do more; militants down South hallucinated he would do *far* more. One group thought he'd try for New York City; the other thought he would reach it! In Lee's eyes, movement that far would be an impossibility; a stupid impossibility, in fact. And his special plan was incredible enough without adding wishful campaigns and conquests. He kept his plan top, top secret.

The invading Commander was going elsewhere: not Philadelphia, not New York. Not Harrisburg. Not Gettysburg, either. Who had heard of Gettysburg before July 1863? It was a crossroads town. So what? The Army of Northern Virginia was not on a sightseeing trip nor a holiday excursion choosing which road or roads to travel.

Robert Edward Lee would implement his unique plan in a place easily attainable. As well, it was a place from which he could extricate his army readily and head back to Virginia if needed. Somewhere within the three counties—Franklin, Adams, York—he would stay for a brief period to accomplish a psychological deed of unusual political import. And do so without military action, preferably. Unless attacked.

Of course the area would have to be isolated from the rest of the Union for a short time period. The area would be protected by the Army of Northern Virginia which could forage at will in fine-soil country with abundant crops and other resources, because, *as per usual,* Lee expected the Federal Army would be south protecting Washington, D.C. Great expectations are one thing; unverifiable expectations another.

And so General Lee gave orders, in his usual secretive manner, to the commander of his Second Corps, Lt. General Ewell, to go to the "banks of the Susquehanna." Ewell was to seal off the area, effectively detaching it from the Union for a brief time, although not making it part of the Confederate States of America. Lee's motivation was to use the area for the political purpose of attaining peace, so he was aiming for a certain historical site in the American saga's political beginnings, one favored by Southerners more than by Northerners.

The river would prevent whatever Pennsylvania militia might be mustered from seriously attacking the Army of Northern Virginia. The Susquehanna would be a barrier which could be defended skillfully because of its span, at various places a mile or so wide. Significantly, its western bank was advantageously defensive with hills for tens upon tens of miles from north of Harrisburg southeastward to the Mason-Dixon Line into Maryland, all abundantly forested along the stream. Hills would be prime sites for artillery pieces and sharpshooter nests to do their business. Woodlands would shield his forces from any action by enemy troops on the lower, more level and open spaces on the east side of the Susquehanna.

"I think your best course will be toward the Susquehanna. ... If Harrisburg comes within your means, capture it," Lee told Ewell on 22 June 1863.[4] "Lee wanted Ewell chiefly to replenish his corps' supplies and remedy its hunger; he permitted Ewell to strike toward Harrisburg, but did not order it outright."[5] Harrisburg was optional.

It was vintage Lee: a discretionary decree. *"If"* may be yes. *"If"* may be no. It depended on whatever Lt. General Ewell thought. It was conditional and not mandatory, because Harrisburg was *not* the place Lee wanted to use as a platform to proclaim peace. Capturing a Northern state capital had no outstanding merit just as the North's actual capital of Washington didn't have urgent merit for the South to seize, so it never attacked Washington, D.C. and there was no need to capture a state capital such as Harrisburg.

But, *if* all went well Ewell may capture it. Harrisburg could be of value *if* Ewell thought it was worth it, but apparently Lee didn't think it necessary so it need not be attacked. What, *if* anything, could be of value in a political capital? Seized governors, captured legislators were not prized, then as now.

The northern section of Ewell's corps went from Chambersburg to the northeast entering the upper reaches of York County to plug up the area where a bridge at Harrisburg crossed the Susquehanna. The Confederate Second Corps commander would make sure that any forces that might be mustered to enter York County from the north would be stopped. Whether or not that bridge was to be burned is moot because nothing is recorded about it.

Meanwhile the southern section of Ewell's corps led by Major General Jubal Early went eastward from Chambersburg to Gettysburg, but stopped at Caledonia on the way. There Early, as per usual, disobeyed Commanding General Lee's order *not* to destroy civilian property. Jubal Early burned down all the buildings of Thaddeus Steven's iron works because it was Representative Stevens who was a Radical Republican of the group that wanted to exact an exceedingly heavy price from the people and states in rebellion. "Early revealed himself as a headstrong ... leader who had the temerity to defy orders whenever he thought fit ... [His] conduct in burning the furnace, saw mill, and two forges, and a rolling mill at Caledonia was rank insubordination."[6] To his great credit General Lee later commanded his commissary officer to provide supplies to the 200 workmen at the Caledonia Iron Works so that they not needlessly suffer—a real contrast of character to the erratic Early. Early was always in bad odor, and remained so his whole life.

On 26 June General Early entered Gettysburg and requisitioned 500 hats, provisions of many sorts and 1,000 pairs of shoes. Or else $10,000 in United States currency. The town leaders pled poverty, for no shoe factory was there, contrary to the fable that had sprung up in the line of march and got puffed up after the war. The fable was that the Rebels went to Gettysburg for shoes, thus lost a battle.

That fable is like a child's lie: an untruth, but fascinating to hear. And, since a spectacular battle occurred in that small crossroads town in homey, rural America the fable is intriguing to hear. Though unreal it appeals to the ear.

But like many fables, it does have "shoes." They still walk in the twenty-first century! People believe the fable of Gettysburg shoes. Grown people love their fables as much as children love theirs, and adults' fables are hoary as Methuselah, and just as surreal.

Early left Gettysburg heading eastward to York. He was to meet Major General Jeb Stuart's cavalry coming into York County from the south *via* Maryland. Stuart first rode around the rear of the Federal army while it was in Virginia and Maryland but did not report its presence to Lee nor to Lt. General James Longstreet as he had been instructed to do. Jeb Stuart's silence affected the battle that was about to happen *accidentally* at Gettysburg, as much as did Lee's silence.

In the process of moving northward Stuart gave the frights to Federals as he raided locales close to Washington, D.C. and then near Baltimore, capturing 125 Union army wagons with many supplies. He made the mistake of dragging them along; he had already destroyed 168 wagons in his escapade and should have destroyed more. All those captured wagons slowed his advance into Pennsylvania. They affected his ability to win a large cavalry skirmish at Hanover in York County. There, a Union sharpshooter zeroed in on an Confederate officer and killed him, the first Rebel blood shed on Union soil in a military engagement of the war.

Meanwhile Early's action through the center of York County ended in the voluntary surrender of York, which resulted in many commandeered supplies for his troops. And cash, always cash—more than $28,000 in United States greenbacks, of course. Thereafter, Early sent Brigadier General John Gordon's brigade farther east to the Susquehanna, to the bridge over the Susquehanna.

It was a magnificent bridge. "The bridge was one mile and a quarter in length" as Early described it, "the superstructure being of wood, on stone pillars, and it included in one structure a railroad bridge, a pass-way for wagons, and also as tow path for the canal, which ... crosses the Susquehanna."[7]

Some 5,620 feet long and twenty-eight feet wide, standing on twenty-seven stone piers and with a carriageway and a walkway, the Wrightsville bridge originally had two towpaths. The paths provided firm footing for draft animals to draw canal boats across the river thus connecting a canal on the Lancaster side (east) and a canal on the York side (west.)

Tolls for the bridge were $1 for a wagon with 6 horses and 6 cents per pedestrian. Its roof was shingled, the sides weather-boarded, the interior whitewashed. In 1846 a double-track railway was added, linking major railroads in Lancaster and York. Because sparks from locomotives could start fires, the rail cars were pulled across the bridge by mules or horses. Privately owned and operated, it was considered the longest covered bridge in the world.

General Early continuing his bastardizing ways and disobeyed Lee's order. The orders were issued through his corps commander, General Ewell. An order that he, Early, himself clearly described in his report about the campaign:

[My] division remained in camp of the 25th [June 1863] and I visited General Ewell at Chambersburg, and received from him instructions to cross South Mountain to Gettysburg, and then proceed to York, and cut the Northern Central Railroad running from Baltimore to Harrisburg, and also *destroy the bridge across the Susquehanna at Wrightsville and Columbia,* on the branch road from York toward Philadelphia, … [8]

And *defiantly* he wrote about his defiance of orders:

I regretted very much the failure to secure this bridge, as finding the defenseless condition of the country and the little obstacle likely to be afforded by the [local] militia to our progress, I had determined if I could get possession of the [Wrightsville] bridge to cross my division over the Susquehanna, and cut the Pennsylvania Central Railroad, march upon Lancaster, lay the town under contribution and then attack Harrisburg in the rear while it *should be attacked* in the front by the rest of the corps, … The project, however, was entirely thwarted by the destruction of the bridge, as the river was otherwise impassible, being very wide and deep at this point.[9]

By Lee's orders the bridge was to have been destroyed. The nugget of historical gold indicates that General Lee was about more than a battle such as the one that resulted at Gettysburg. His plan called for York County obviously to be isolated. The area was to be shielded by destruction of that bridge on the east side of the county while screened on the north side by the main body of Second Corps, Army of Northern Virginia. And *if* and only *if* Harrisburg came within Ewell's means—easy means at that because there was *not* to be combat, a general battle, unless attacked—to capture the capital of the Keystone State.

Indubitably the Wrightsville/Columbia bridge was to be destroyed whereas a sub-sub-commander made up his mind to disobey his commanding general's order. He would supersede his commanding general's plan with his own. Again indubitably, it was "rank insubordination" on Early's part—except that he was saved by some Northerners who beat him to the punch and burned the magnificent bridge themselves.

Moreover, with brazen indignity, Early stated categorically that Harrisburg *should* have been attacked—thereby reprimanding his commanders. The action was true to his character. It was well known in the Confederate military that Early was a faultfinder. Often he rendered razor-edged criticisms of his subordinates, but this statement was blatant opposition to a superior officer's plan.

In time, March 1865, Lee wrote to Early that he had to relieve him of his command because "I could not oppose what seems to be the current of opinion, … I therefore felt constrained … to find a commander who would be more likely to develop the strength and resources of the country, and inspire the soldiers with confidence." A duty-breaker does not develop the strength and resources of a country nor does a duty-breaker inspire confidence. In the end, Jubal Early's insubordination was recorded, officially.

No wonder then that Jubal Early fled after the war to Mexico, then Cuba, then Canada. Who would want a former officer who broke the rules and disobeyed his commander? Later returning to the re-united States, he became the nineteenth-century super-adulator of Robert E. Lee. Jubal Early appeared to think that if he would shine honor super-abundantly and redundantly on Lee that he himself *ipso facto* would be illuminated and acclaimed.

True, Robert Lee's prominence increased. Jubal, however, became a cutesy name in post-war America, and non-existent today. Early attempted to cover his deficiencies with adulation of Lee, bad enough because contrary to Robert E, Lee's character. But Early took to super-adulation of the modest ex-general. Lee didn't need ballooning of any sort. And "Robert Lee" is a name given to scores of male babies.

The Wrightsville/Columbia bridge at the center of the controversy burned brightly. The Pennsylvania militia used oil to fire the bridge since the explosive charges set off failed to "shiver the timber" the Union commander aimed at; not enough to drop the fourth span from the Wrightsville side into the river, and simply "render the bridge useless to the enemy."[10] Had the dynamite charges exploded properly there would have been a 200-foot wide gap in the bridge, not its total destruction, which finally happened. It was a drastic measure that had to be used so the Confederates couldn't capture the bridge. Northern forces burned the magnificent bridge.

What preceded the burning was complete unease and dark trepidation. Major Granville Haller of the Seventh U. S. Infantry reported:

> The troops from York under my charge arrived at Wrightsville about 7:30 PM. A scene presented itself which can hardly be exaggerated. Locomotives, tenders, and cars of all description lined the railroad awaiting removal to Columbia [on the east bank.]

> The turnpike road [from York] leading to the bridge was lined with large wagons removing property of citizens across the Susquehanna. There was much time lost by teamsters having to halt and pay toll … I sought Dr. [Barton] Evans, president of the bridge company, and pointed out the detention at the bridge and the removal of the people being involuntary, urged that tolls should not be exacted. The president at once threw the bridge open to traffic free.[11]

The conflagration that followed ignition dumped much of the bridge in the river. After the war the Federal government wouldn't pay a penny to rebuild it, again neglecting the soft-underbelly region of the North. In war it seems only the enemy deserves attention.

Near the end, as noted, Lee's order to burn the bridge was executed—by Yankees. Yankees who didn't know they were fulfilling General Lee's order!

York County was isolated, but only halfway. At Wrightsville the wide Susquehanna blocked off intrusion from the east with its long, commodious bridge in fiery embers over twenty-seven stone piers, railroad tracks twisted while the numerous huge support timbers burned for days.

Farther north the Second Corps, ANV had failed; it never got to

Harrisburg. Scouts saw the city from about five miles away. The main body of the Corps heard about Harrisburg from a distance of eleven miles or so. However, sightseeing wasn't scouts' duty, and tales of a river city aren't illuminating, at all, to footsloggers who want rest.

With little delay, the action planned by Robert E. Lee moved backwards, to Adams County in the soft underbelly of the North. There, at an undistinguished crossroad country town, two armies surprised each other.

Chapter Notes

1. Tony Horwitz. Midnight Rising: John Brown and the Raid That Sparked the Civil War (N.Y.: Henry Holt, 2011): 170.
2. Ethan Sepp Rafuse. Robert E. Lee And The Fall Of The Confederacy, 1863-65 (Landham and Littlefield, 2008): 37. (Emphases in original)
3. Clifford Dowdey and Louis H. Manarin (Eds.) The Wartime Papers of R. E. Lee. (Boston: Little, Brown, 1961): 411.
4. WR/OR. I. 27. 3. 914.
5. David J. Eicher. The Longest Night: A Military History of the Civil War (N.Y.: Simon & Schuster, 2001): 506.
6. Edwin Coddington. The Gettysburg Campaign: A Study in Command (N.Y.: Touchstone Simon & Schuster, 1997): 166.
7. WR/OR. I. 27. 2. 467.
8. Ibid., 464-65. (Emphasis added)
9. Ibid. 467. (Emphasis added)
10. Ibid. 996.
11. Ibid., 995.

CHAPTER 19

"A Crown for York!"*

* *Third Part of Henry VI.* 1. 4. 94. William Shakespeare

WHAT CAN BE said about York? Two things, authentically; one negative, one positive.

Socrates of ancient Athens provides the prime technique for analyzing how the negative and positive of something ought to be presented. One first starts with the negative; that is to root out, plow up, harrow intellectual soil, preparing it for conceptual seed planting. Then when sufficient work has been done, one follows with the positive, that is, to plant, cultivate, nurture our intellectual soil and harvest the fruits of labor.

The positive of York comes from the time of the national origin of the United States of America. When the colonies were being united as states, York stood tall. The negative of York comes from the time when the United States of America was struggling to save the nation from being dis-united. When the states were in the process of dis-union, York slunk away in shame.

Analyzing the negative and positive of York excavates flakes of gold with potential to enlarge our understanding of history.

The Negative of York

Before the negative be told, there was something of worth in York during the war to preserve the Union, but no thanks are due Yorkers.

The year before the Gettysburg battle, the Sixth Cavalry from New York State erected barracks on Penn Common in York, land donated by the William Penn family. The barracks were transformed into the U. S. Army General Hospital to serve wounded soldiers from field hospitals in Virginia. It opened in June 1862, and three months later served the wounded from both armies after the battle of Antietam in Maryland, 80 miles away. Yorkers had little to do with the hospital; it was as much an intrusion in their lives as a good for fellow human beings.

However, the outright negative about York is its surrender to the Rebels—the only Northern community to surrender! York, in fact, did not resist surrender.

The surrender was ignominious. York gave in, gave up, caved in, backed down, threw in the towel, knuckled under—say it as you will—and paid in cash and commodities to do so!

At the heart of York's surrender is an infamous act.

Its shameful *action of inaction* was not out of agreement with the Southern cause. No, York surrendered out of the prevailing culture's apathy, that is the culture of the Pennsylvania Dutch. That amorphous, bland, detached, equivocal, non-committal attitude dominated the town authorities, who were considered "the English," meaning persons not of German heritage.

If one does not want to accept the inaction as shameful and wants to put a positive spin on the unsatisfactory behavior of the capitulators and how the surrender happened, one can say it was Pennsylvania Dutch pragmatism. "We saved ourselves to fight another day" sounds reasonable. "Toh-MAY-toh or toh-MAH-toh," call York's capitulation pragmatic or call it incomprehensible, it was shabby self-justification all the same.

The truth is no one can know with certainty the real reason for York's surrender because it, too, has been missing much like the Confederate planning records of May 1863 for the Northern Campaign of the Army of Northern Virginia. However, there was a "good" reason for surrender given at the time by the Committee of Safety formed in York 15 June 1863, two weeks before the Battle of Gettysburg. That reason? No troops were available to defend the town.

The Committee of Safety didn't mention that citizens weren't willing to fight for their town or nation. Actually, few people cared to know why they didn't fight. Surrender was the "wise" course of action.

The York Committee of Safety had been organized in order to prepare to meet the Southern invaders two counties to the west, in Franklin County. The committee met Saturday, 27 June 1863 at 7:30 p.m. In its one act of "defiance," it voted to raise Old Glory in Continental Square, York. It was a magical thinking, an act to cover something else, as if a piece of cloth could drive away the invaders. It was an act of faith—"bad faith," that is.

> RESOLVED: That finding our town defenseless we request the Chief Burgess to *surrender* the town peacefully and to obtain for us the assurance that the persons of citizens and private property should be respected, the Chief Burgess to be accompanied by such of the Committee as may think proper to join him.[1]

The sub-committee which joined the Chief Burgess was composed of three of the fifteen members of the Committee of Safety who "thought proper" to accompany him. Only three! A meager show of support. Additionally, a prominent industrialist, Arthur Farquhar, volunteered himself as a public representative to meet the Rebels. To protect his prosperous local industry? We'll never know: records are missing here, too.

The Committee of Safety met with urgency. So pressing was the situation that the committee gave only half an hour for an interchange of ideas or suggestions or argumentation! With much ado the meeting was punctuated by the sub-committee's leave-taking at 8 o'clock the same Saturday evening. Were secret meetings held afore time to minimize discussion? Was short shrift given to people who might fight the invader?

Half an hour to discuss meeting the enemy? Sounds just about right: about the right amount of time to cave in to fear with wimpish behavior. Pragmatism is powerful justification for just about any action, reaction, inaction in the world; it covers a heap and a horde of misbehaviors. Often pragmatism is trivial and trumpery.

Five men set out from York to meet an army. One could think their action was a courageous repetition of the Biblical story of brave David going out to meet the giant Goliath. One would be wrong. To use the anglicized Pennsylvania Dutch colloquialism, they "hiked their heinies" out of town *post haste* westward on the York/Gettysburg Pike. Not to meet the enemy, not to bargain with them, not to reason with them, and positively not to stand and fight. They pled impotence! Testosterone was in thimble supply on the road from York to Gettysburg. Patriotism? It joined the angels on the head of a pin.

Five, to meet thousands of Early's division with Brigidier General John Gordon in the lead before it got to York? The scene was nowhere close to heroism. It revealed: Self-centeredness.

They may have thought they were going to meet the enemy to show patriotism. If so, it would have been inscrutable patriotism. Indeed, in York on 28 June 1863 there wasn't a David. There were goldbrickers. Slouches, bystanders, and sell-outs, too.

At its best, the charade was passivity.

General Gordon assured them of the protection they asked. Furthermore, he stated *as per their request*, "that there was nothing [to be] said by either party about a *surrender* of the town."[2] The five emissaries, speaking on behalf of the fifteen-member Committee of Safety, had the gall to ask that the word *surrender* not be used to describe the surrender. What patriotism! Inscrutable indeed. Cowardice likes words.

The Confederate forces arrived in York on Sunday morning about ten o'clock as worshippers were entering Trinity German Reformed Church, just off Centre Square, on the main east-west route through town connecting Gettysburg to the Susquehanna River at Wrightsville. The church bells were ringing a message that might have been interpreted by the Confederates as a welcome. It surely wasn't a call for resistance: not on "the Lord's Day" for good Christian folk.

> The whole population soon thronged the streets, and men, women and children looked with curious eyes, mingled with undefined apprehensions, upon the motley procession of cavalry, infantry and artillery marching up Market Street, the soldiers looking curiously from side to side, astonished not less at their observers than their observers were at them. The people were in holiday or Sunday costume, the ladies in all their fashionable finery, and the men looking well dressed and comfortable, in strange contrast with the ragged and worn appearance of the invading army. These first troops that entered the town were Gen. Gordon's brigade of 2,500 men, [which] marched up Market Street and on toward Wrightsville. The Union flag was floating in the centre square and was taken down and carried off by them.[3]

A more illustrative picture of Yorkers' acceptance of the surrender was drawn by a Southern officer. Lieutenant Robert Stiles noted an unhesitating acceptance had not been expected from the surrendering citizens.

> [Then as] we were entering York, General William T. Smith [was leading our regiment.] The population seemed to be in the streets, and I saw General Smith—we called him "Old Governor"—had blood in his eyes. Turning to his aide, he told him to "go back to those 'tooting' fellows," as he called the brigade band, "and tell them to march into town tooting *Yankee Doodle*.

> The band got to the head of the column and struck up *Yankee Doodle*. The Old Governor, riding alone and bareheaded in front, began bowing and saluting first to one side and then

the other, and especially every pretty girl he saw, with that manly, hearty smile which no man or woman ever resisted. The Yorkers seemed at first astounded, then pleased, and finally, by the time we reached the public square, they broke into enthusiastic cheers, till the Old Governor called a halt.

It was a rare scene—the vanguard of an invading army and the invading population hobnobbing on the public green in an enthusiastic gathering.[4]

Division commander General Early proceeded to occupy the county court house which could be used later by General Lee—conceivably for what later would be called by a Richmond newspaper his *"grandest, wisest, most imposing scheme ever."* Early had noted the richness of the surrounding farmland, the industrial prosperity of the town with its railroad shops and various mechanical businesses, and the acquiescence of the citizenry. Then, based upon his overall perception of the community, he made his demands. Of course he wanted Federal money, the sum of $100,000. He got less than he stipulated—the populace was, after all, frugal Pennsylvania Dutch for whom wealth was a sign of God's blessing, to be kept by the one "who got it."

And then they thought they pulled a sharp one on the Rebels: $28,000. Not $100,000. Like Little Jack Horner sitting in a corner eating his Christmas pie, who stuck in his thumb and pulled out a plum and said what a good boy am I—but what has a plum to do with goodness! What has $72,000 "saved" to do with patriotism?

What Early did get he accepted promptly. Both exacting "guest" and complying "hosts" were pleased with their childish bargain.

The plunder amassed 1,000 hats, 1,000 pairs of socks, 2,000 pairs of boots and shoes. Early was presented with a bonanza, liberally given: 22,000 pounds of beef, 3,500 pounds of sugar, 1,200 pounds of salt, 165 barrels of flour, 300 gallons of molasses, and 1,650 pounds of coffee. It looked as if the town were making ready for the coming Fourth of July shindig celebrating American independence from Mother England.

Nonetheless, Jubal was jubilant. No wonder: Federal dollars down south were far more valuable than their own hyperinflated Dixienotes. The sum $28,610 would be worth more than $100,000 in Confederate currency.[5] The money plundered would have tremendous worth given the easy and widespread counterfeiting of Confederate grayback bills. Counterfeiting alone could have defeated the Confederacy. Southern inflation was so massive that finally printing money became too costly to be profitable, and they stopped it. The "graybacks" couldn't pay for themselves! Northern greenbacks to the tune of $28,610 were a king's ransom—a.k.a. a cowards' sellout.

The York scene in 1863—null Federal military presence, abundantly fruitful agriculture, productive industry, minimal population, plentiful horseflesh to ride, pork, chicken, beef, turkey to eat, plus tasty German pastries, German beer to guzzle, all around pleasant scenery and waterways, *and* a laid-back citizenry willing to cooperate—was a fine place for a mystery tour on the part of the Confederacy.

Early's captured York countians were mystified.

As a conquered people they brooded over questions important to them at the time: Who are these poorly garbed yet disciplined soldiers? Conquerors, but respectful at the same time? What do they want? Where are they going? *Vas gibt's mit diese Rebellen?* What's happening next? Where is the famous General Lee? Why did he send thousands of troops to our bucolic countryside? How come the weird hand signals sold to us by (unscrupulous) hucksters of fear did not work to protect us from the invaders?

They lamented that weeks had passed since Lee had crossed into Pennsylvania. Where are our Union troops? They've had ample time since Lee crossed into Pennsylvania to get here. Where are they? Why this Confederate attention to York?

"Stonewall" Jackson would have been pleased: "Mystery, mystery is the secret of success."[6] Mystification was intense in surrendered

York. Citizens were flummoxed—perhaps *verhexed!* They believed in *hexing,* bewitching, so were ripe for mystification.

Something more was going to happen. But what?

"Surrender" answered the question sufficiently for Yorkers in 1863.

The Positive of York

The positive thing about York is huge. York had a crown in its past, a patriotic crowning that few places in the United States of America had or have. Lee would capitalize on it: York had been a Capital of the United States of America.

York became the seat of the American government in October 1777 when Continental Congress fled from the British army that was occupying Philadelphia during the Revolutionary War. Congressmen wanted the Susquehanna River, eighty miles west of Philadelphia, between themselves and Redcoats; the river was a barrier. Congressmen journeyed like a couple about to give birth to a new child where they could rest, recuperate, and bring into the world something new. So the Second Continental Congress of the United States traveled another eleven miles west of the river to York, variously called York Town or Yorktown, even Little York to differentiate if from "big" New York.

York was the capital while the Continental Army commanded by General George Washington wintered at Valley Forge in 1777-78, sorely testing whether it, and the whole American revolution, would survive or die in winter's bitter cold.

Rather than the dunce's hat that York later plunked on its own head in the June 1863 surrender, York in 1777-78 had worn a revolutionary crown.

York's Revolutionary War past stood out in four significant events that materialized in the town, which probably influenced R. E. Lee's choice of place.

One: The governing body for the thirteen colonies, the Continental Congress, enacted a formal document indicating the nature of the new government, in York. Two: The reaffirmation of the masterful

Virginian, George Washington, as leader of the American opposition to Great Britain, took place there. Three: York was the locale in the United States of America where the nation took its place formally and diplomatically among the world's nations through ambassadorial recognition of its very existence. Four: An interesting prisoner of war camp during the American Revolution was located there, having an aftermath in the next century.

And, unexpectedly to this account, there may be a reason from the War of 1812—when Lee was a boy of five years—that caused him as an adult to choose York to perform a significant act.

York's *premier* event from the Revolutionary War was the creation of the first founding constitution of American governance: the Articles of Confederation and Perpetual Union. Benjamin Franklin, though not present nor a member of that particular Continental Congress in York, was the most evident influence on the framers of the document. He had proposed that seminal idea with the title Articles of Confederation and Perpetual Union to the Continental Congress of May 1775 in Philadelphia. Although that Congress did not act on his proposal, various of his proposed articles were adopted into that first constitution of the United States of America promulgated at York. It started:

> Whereas the Delegates of the United States of America, in Congress assembled, did, on the 15th day of November, in the Year of Our Lord One thousand Seven Hundred and Seventy seven, and in the Second Year of the Independence of America, agree to certain articles of Confederation and perpetual Union between the States of New-hampshire, Massachusetts-bay, Rhodeisland and Providence Plantations, Connecticut, New York, New Jersey, Pennsylvania, Delaware, Maryland, Virginia, North-Carolina, South-Carolina, and Georgia in the words following, viz. "Articles of Confederation and perpetual Union between the states of New-hampshire, Massachusetts-bay, Rhodeisland and Providence Plantations, Connecticut, New-York, New-Jersey, Pennsylvania, Delaware, Maryland, Virginia, North-Carolina, South-Carolina and Georgia."

The document was signed by forty-eight Revolutionary luminaries among whom the brightest were John Hancock, Samuel Adams, Elbridge Gerry, Francis Dana, Richard Henry Lee, Robert Morris, Roger Sherman, John Witherspoon, Gouvenor Morris, Henry Laurens, and Francis Lightfoot Lee.

America lived with the propositions of the Articles of Confederation and Perpetual Union from 1777 until the present Constitution was adopted in 1789. The United States of America was a confederacy at its birth as a government. That First Confederacy continued longer than the short-lived confederacy that endured for only four years during the war from 1861-65. Southerners tried to establish a confederacy without a perpetual union and it cost 620,000 human lives and the Southern economy for a century.

The content within that first constitution proved inadequate for governance of the new nation, of course. "The United States in Congress assembled" depended on states to fund the government through requisition requests and not direct taxation. But states are as individualistic as their citizens. At different times for different reasons some states did not heed the monetary requisitions so the first American government was stymied, even stopped from governing. States in several instances went their own ways taking maverick latitude to themselves in the Perpetual Union. Thus, "a more pefect Union" had to be stated and organized in the second (and present) constitution of 1787.

At best the First Confederacy was a noble inspiration; at worst it was feeble as any newborn. Its central government was hardly a government at all. In fact the weak central government of the Articles had to vie for power with thirteen separate state governments. States guarded their provincial, even parochial, rights to the detriment of the national government and to the Perpetual Union. It was a recipe for failure.

The states were as narcissistic as every newborn baby, the center of its own universe. Very few Americans could stomach perpetual babyhood and few mourned the passing of the First Confederacy. It died, ill-proportioned and warped almost from birth.

The same kind of provincialism and parochialism infested the second Confederacy and aided its quicker demise.

In the mix, two of Lee's distinguished forebears, his grandfather and grand-uncle, had, at York, argued for and signed the Articles of Confederation and Perpetual Union. Surely Robert E. Lee's heart-strings would have resonated with his forbears, for human dead and their principles tug at our human hearts, resembling our resonance with our living peers.

Regardless of the First Confederacy's downfall, its place of origin would have had an honest historical attraction for Robert E. Lee. There he could present the cause of peace to both the Confederate States of America and the United States of America.

The *second* important event that happened at York was clouded by a desire *not* to harm George Washington, not to diminish respect for him among the citizenry. Its presentation therefore has been muted in historical records. It occurred at a lodging house in York alongside the Plough Tavern, both places frequented by members of Congress. In those buildings, now preserved, Congressmen and military men took their respite, meals, and lodging during Congressional sessions.

The war had not been going well, as noted by the movement of the revolutionary capital. Continental Congress escaped ninety or so miles westward, from Philadelphia to York, to avoid capture by the British army.

General Washington couldn't do anything about that army. As a victorious commander-in-chief he was not faring well; a string of losses plagued him. On the other hand Major General Horatio Gates had had several victories with an important one at Saratoga, New York. His army forced the significant British army of General Burgoyne to surrender on 17 October 1777. That defeat stopped the British attempt to cut off New England from the mid-Atlantic and southern colonies, thus preventing the country from being split asunder.

During the turbulent times, Continental Congress and George Washington were never kissing cousins. Seldom did the general get the help and supplies from Congress he requested for his army, as noted in the terrible experience at Valley Forge that winter of 1777-78. There were simmering animosities between civilian congressmen and the military commander, such as the one allowing General Gates to send reports directly to Congress, bypassing his superior officer, Commander-in-Chief General Washington.

A coterie of supporters of General Gates sought to take advantage of Gates' Saratoga victory and Washington's movements backwards. A "Gates man," Brigadier General Thomas Conway previously served 20 years in the French army. He wrote to General Gates that Washington was a "weak general" and that he considered Gates to be top-commander material.

Over Washington's disapproval, Continental Congress made Conway a Major General in December 1777 and named him Inspector General of the whole Continental army. Trouble definitely was in the making for the American Commander-in-Chief; he was at sixes and sevens with Congress and fellow officers.

Apparently General Conway encouraged a band of like-minded officers to hold a celebration in the Plough Tavern to honor General Horatio Gates, suggesting Gates be lionized as a great commander. One can imagine that in the politico-military atmosphere of York at the time, such a bold operation could not be kept quiet.

During the celebration on 31 January 1778 as fluids flowed, events were exaggerated as boasts ballooned, the twenty-one-year-old Marquis de Lafayette arose suddenly, offered a toast to George Washington, Commander-in-Chief. That's all, no further words of explanation.

What to do? The gathered men could not but raise their glasses in tribute to the Virginian.

Major General Lafayette, the youthful Frenchman, had surprised them all. His simple toast toppled the bid to topple Washington. The "Conway Cabal" was the only attempt to displace Washington in that years-long revolution. Later General Gates apologized, as a gentleman would, to Washington for his part in the thwarted muddle.

Thomas Conway resigned his commission, and in the summer of 1778 was wounded in a duel. After his physical recovery, he recovered his sanity, too. He put his apology to General Washington on paper and returned to France. Whether or not he took for his services any "continentals," the barely solvent American currency, is not known.

George Washington was saved politically in York at the worst time in his career by a young foreign officer who volunteered—serving without pay—to help throw off tyranny. When Washington was President of the United States of America, the Marquis de Lafayette visited York two times, for no known governmental reason or political advantage of note. Human beings like to revisit their fields of glory.

In the next century at his parental home, "Washington and Washington memorabilia were a part of Robert Lee's everyday experience."[6] The aged Marquis de LaFayette, who had been a personal friend of General Washington, in 1824 made a triumphant tour of the States—a year before Robert Lee entered West Point. The Marquis visited the Lee home in Alexandria, Virginia. There he paid homage to his war time friend, General Harry Lee, talked with Anna, wife of "Light-Horse Harry," and was inspirational to their son, Robert Edward.

The stories about York and Lee, Lafayette and Washington make good legends, better by far than the Washington fables about truth-telling, an ax to a cherry tree and not lying about it, or references to strength like throwing a silver dollar across the Potomac river—years before silver dollars were ever minted!

The *third* significant event that took place in York in the Revolutionary War era concerns the struggling nation's standing against the largest army and navy at the time. The event pertains to America's place in the sun, a place at the table of nations and before the bar of international law. America—composed of ordinary tradesmen, seamstresses, farmers, lawyers, midwifes, cobblers, butchers, sawyers, firefighters, merchants, charwomen, soldiers, drovers, tailors, physicians, craftspeople, scribes, coachmen, backwoodsmen, cooks, printers, carpenters, policemen, blacksmiths, dentists, sailors, planters, coopers, shopkeepers, draymen, weavers, bakers, teachers, clothiers, and all other diverse creators of goods— received official diplomatic recognition as a free and independent nation.

France stood up against Britannia's power. It gave diplomatic recognition to the United States of America. At that moment, America belonged. We became a nation among nations. Seemingly no more than a formality, nonetheless diplomatic status assured the legitimacy of our revolt against the tyranny of the English king, George III. France pledged that it would stand with us to the end.

The French monarchy was true to its word. France sent thousands of soldiers and sailors to aid America in our War of Independence after it declared war on Great Britain. Factually, nearly an equal number of French and American ground combatants fought in the war-ending battle of Yorktown in 1781. If one also counts the sailors in the French fleet of twenty-four men-of-war that defeated the British fleet of nineteen at the mouth of the Chesapeake Bay, our French ally's total commitment would have outnumbered Americans fighting for independence. The British had 7,247 men at Yorktown.[7] The Americans about 9,000. Our French allies supplied 11,000 soldiers, marines, and sailors at Yorktown. The French aristocrat, Gilbert du Motier, Marquis de LaFayette, age twenty-four, who served America without pay, had badgered the British army before General Washington showed on the scene. As expected, the young major general was effective in the ultimate surrender of Cornwallis at Yorktown.

It's no wonder then that years later when American troops landed in France to help fight Germany in World War I, the American declaration was, "Lafayette, we are here!" America was repaying a debt.

The *fourth* thing to be said about York in the Revolutionary War period had little import in that time. It became important when the great wave of immigrants came to the growing America in the 1820s and thereafter, so many from Germany, so many that in the twenty-first century, Americans with German backgrounds are the largest element of the American population. Continental Congress had set up a prisoner of war camp on the eastern edge of York for captured British troops and named it Camp Security. Also among the imprisoned were some German mercenary troops serving the English.

Those mercenaries had been employed by the British crown because its royal line came from the Hannover area of Germany. In fact, the British monarch, George III, was also the Elector, the ruler, of Hannover and recruited troops from Germany to fight in his wars. Most of the mercenaries came from Hesse. He paid $150,000 to other German princes for the service of 30,067 "Hessians." Of that number 12,562 did not return to Germany, including 7,754 who died in America. There were 4,808 living Hessians who remained in America—to become American citizens. And to invite other Germans to the land of freedom's holy light.

After the Revolutionary War various of those remaining 4,808 stayed in York County or other great farming areas such as Lancaster County, across the river. Others moved westward to the frontier in Appalachia and the Mississippi Valley. Those ex-soldiers, now newly minted Americans, communicated with people back home about the verdant land in America. The Hessians who settled in Pennsylvania were among the forerunners of the Pennsylvania Dutch, enticing Germans from the Hesse area to settle in a peaceful place, a veritable Beulah land "of corn and wine, all riches freely mine." Southcentral Pennsylvania became a safe haven for Germans *en masse* for the next six decades up to the North-South conflict.

What happened in Revolutionary York lent authenticity and authority to the place for R. E. Lee to engage in psychological warfare by proposing peace at the original seat of the First Confederacy.

However, catching us totally off guard, R. E. Lee may have had created for him a deeply personal relationship with York. It dated back to the War of 1812, some 29 years after the Revolutionary War.

His father, General "Light Horse Harry" Lee, close friend of President Washington and outstanding cavalry commander in the Southern states during the War of the Revolution, was in Baltimore, Maryland the summer of 1812. Lee's father strongly supported freedom of the press by siding with and visiting the editor of the *Federal Republican* newspaper who robustly opposed the War of 1812, called "Mr. Madison's War." A mob ferociously attacked the newspaper and the people who defended the editor. A mob murdered a defender, Revolutionary War colleague General James Lingan, tarred and feathered John Thompson, and viciously beat and knifed General "Light Horse Harry" Lee, before pouring hot candle wax in his eye and leaving him for dead.

An affidavit before a Justice of the Peace, Montgomery County, Maryland on 12 August 1812 noted that "General Lee was taken to the hospital where his wounds were dressed by physicians ... Hence he was next conveyed to the country and arrived at Little York, Pennsylvania, where he is said to be doing well."[8]

John Thompson wrote a narrative on 6 August 1812, "After the crowd had dispersed, some of my friends who did not think me safe sent me a carriage into which I was put, without losing a minute, and General [Light Horse Harry] Lee was put in the same carriage. We were hurried into the country in our wounded, bruised, and mangled condition; we arrived in Yorktown, Pennsylvania on Saturday evening, the first of August, where we received humane and friendly sympathies and attentions of the inhabitants, and the medical aid of two gentlemen of the faculty."[9]

Though his father deserted the family after the Baltimore mob attacks, the boy, Robert E. Lee, may have remembered graphically what he had heard had happened to his father. No evidence exists indicating that the young Lee repudiated his father nor eviscerated his memory with forgetfulness. As well, given the nature of his humanity it is likely the younger Lee would have remembered Yorkers as humane, friendly, sympathetic, and medical benefactors. He may have viewed them as Good Samaritans, neighbors to a man who fell among mobsters, cutthroats and murderers.

R. E. Lee may have been going to York to repay a family debt.

He was literate enough to have known York's history. He would have seen worth for the South in capitalizing on its historical import and its compassionate past. The occupation of York would ring political bells in the South if used aright in psychological warfare.

York was a 24-carat prize in the geographical area, perfectly suited for an epiphany, an unveiling, a new way of beholding reality. "Stonewall" would have been ecstatic to be part of the supreme surprise that "peace, not combat," was the content of Lee's plan and intent of the invasion. Jackson had written to his wife Mary Anna on 11 April 1862, a year before he died and thus before the bloody loss at Gettysburg, that he was weary of war. "I do hope that the war will soon be over, and that I shall never again be called upon to take the field."

Proposing peace at York would give rise to an epiphany in a new way. It would be presented by a military officer, not a politician, a military officer who would not be wanton and attack for attack's sake or for supremacy, destroying civilians and their property thoughtlessly. It would be a way not heralded by special interest groups such as slaveholders or Abolitionists, not office-holders or aristocrats, not Capital or Labor. A military officer esteemed on both sides of the Mason-Dixon Line would set out a road map for termination of the fratricidal war.

York would be his chosen site in 1863 as the place for a new beginning to counteract the war's cruelty, its marring of the Republic's very founding, its devastation of God's fair Earth. The simple reason for Lee's choice was that York had had crowning moments in 1777-78—and later—as the setting of precious new beginnings.

The chief basis for going to York would have been the orderly, sanctioned, authoritative formulation of a governing document: the Articles of Confederation and Perpetual Union. The Founding Fathers at that place approved a constitution to provide a formal government of the emerging nation. It had happened in brave and daring—and patriotic—York. Robert Lee could build on that historical distinction.

Ever the astute observer, he would have had his eye on some place to give a psychological advantage for a crowning event, the purpose of his Northern Campaign.

In a near-final analysis, much can be said about York, from nation's capital to national disgrace, from Articles of Confederation and Perpetual Union to Confederate occupation—with positives and negatives, highs and some lows.

There were All-American flakes of gold discoverable in a small American town.

Chapter Notes

1. "PA Civil War: Civil War History in York County, PA" in Pennsylvania Volunteers Of The Civil War on website http://www.pacivilwar.com/county/yorkhistory.html © 1997-2011. Entries concerning 28 June 1863. (Emphasis added)

2. Ibid. (Emphasis added)

3. Ibid.

4. O. Eisenschiml & R. Newman. The Civl War: An American Iliad (N.Y.: Bobbs Merrill Co, 1947): 458-59.

5. See the careful explanation in Money and Finance In The Confederate States Of America by Marc Weidenmier, Claremont McKenna College website http://eh.net/encyclopedia/article/weidenmier.finance.confederacy.us

6. E. B. Pryor. Reading The Man. 51-52.

7. Burke Davis. The Campaign That Won America: The Story of Yorktown (Washinton: Acorn Press/National Park Service, 1979): 275. See also Pp. 306-7 for estimate that the American/French alliance outnumbered the British two-to-one.

8. A Contemporaneous Account of the Baltimore Riot of 1812, Baltimore: 1 September 1812. 34. See: http://penelope.uchicago.edu/Thayer/E/Gazetteer/Topics/history/American_and_Military/1812_Baltimore_Riot/Sep1_1812_pamphlet/Montgomery_County_record*.html

9. Ibid. 47.

CHAPTER 20

Aiming ~~for Gettysburg~~ Elsewhere

"IT IS SCARCELY too much to say that on July 2 [1863] the Army of Northern Virginia was without a commander."[1]

This admission by the chief apologist and preeminent admirer of R. E. Lee is a peculiar yet remarkable particle of historical gold washed down to us. The starkness of the words indicates a vacuity at worst or a crucial error in his idol. Plainly, it is a precious nugget that tells us Lee was "out of it."

All the same, historian Douglas Southall Freeman didn't tell the full story of 1, 2, 3 July '63, even in four volumes. Centering on Gettysburg, one discovers that Robert E. Lee was "out of it" for more than a single day of the battle. As an acute observer would expect, he was "out of it" for a reason.

The story was not an excuse, about Lee's diarrhea—or of berries or some other thing he ate. Nor was it an excuse to say he was anxious; he was functioning with a lack of information from his cavalry commander Jeb Stuart. General Stuart had been sent to scout out for and then meet up with Confederate General Ewell, commander of the Second Corps of the Army of Northern Virginia, when Lee had divided his army in Pennsylvania.

Lee maintained the cavalry was the eyes and ears of his army, to provide him information about the enemy. But if Lee's hardship were only about information, then it is unclear why he couldn't have sent any, and all, of his *other* cavalry units to gather information when

Stuart's units dropped out of contact. Lee had various cavalry units to scout out the Federal army. He didn't send them. He retained belief that his opponents, as usual, would be protecting their capital at Washington. This firmly held belief made him oblivious to the facts on the ground: the Union army was tracking him. The Army of the Potomac sometimes seemingly imagined that Lee's army had vanished, yet the Federals persisted in looking for his Confederate army.

Whatever the misapprehensions on both sides, a question remains about Lee's campaign. Why did he cross the Potomac River and go north again after the lost battle at Antietam/Sharpsburg Maryland just nine months before?

Surely, part of the answer is for supplies, for forage availability in Pennsylvania. Nevertheless, was his action for ego satisfaction, too? After two great victories, Fredericksburg in December 1862 and Chancellorsville in May 1863, did he suppose he could get the same victorious results that superseded the pathetic loss at Antietam in September '62?

On another hand, if his singular purpose were to win an overwhelming victory in a great battle on Northern soil, wouldn't Lee have realized that he would have to backtrack southward? Wouldn't that retrograde action be perceived as a negative, by Northerners—and also Southerners? Lee was an aggressive commander, but was he an illogical gambler looking only one step ahead?

If, as many historians contend, he planned a super-sized, war-ending battle, wouldn't his plan have to have been super-sized itself, with many more troops than he had? Wouldn't he have demanded more troops than ever and not have settled for fewer? More supplies than usual? More top officers drawn from other eastern areas?

And why would he have changed the structure of an army that had been greatly successful in the two previous battles for the—supposed—"mother-of-all battles," to use modern parlance? Why a new organization; three corps in place of two? Thus "compelled to place two-thirds of the troops under corps commanders who had never directed that many men in battle; then it was that the sentimental demand of the South led him to put at the head of the reduced Second Corps [recently Jackson's command] the gallant Ewell who had never served directly under Lee and was unfamiliar with his discretionary methods."[2] Obviously he had to replace the deceased "Stonewall" Jackson, but now he had placed two new officers in charge of his three-corps army. Why three for the first time under his command? Would the two new ones know how to heed his orders—properly?

Wouldn't an all-out, massive, enemy-destroying battle necessitate an almost perfect plan *surpassing* anything he had done before? Wouldn't it require input from other military leaders than "wanna-be General" J. Davis and Inspector General Sam Cooper? What military expertise had the civilian politicians in the Cabinet? Some things— plural—were missing in Robert E. Lee's plan if it were to entail a final battle for a final triumph. The nature of Lee's secret plan was the crux of the matter.

The questions started exploding, beginning in late June when a spy reported that Major General George Meade had replaced "Fighting Joe" Hooker. The appointment was a particular annoyance to Lee, who knew Meade of old from the Mexican-American war. Meade. was different from the other Union generals Lee had outwitted and defeated. Lee noted, "General Meade will commit no blunder on my front, and if I make one he will make haste to take advantage of it."[3] Lee realized fully the implications of not re-fighting his previous opponent, "Fighting Joe" Hooker: Hooker knew how to give up!

The change in Union commanders compromised R. E. Lee's plan. Events around Lee were altering and his grip was loosening on their meaning. Lee was exasperated; it was abysmally disturbing news. He had counted on the Federal army to do what it had done when Confederates maneuvered in proximity to the capital, which is the reason he had wanted "an army in effigy" to freeze the Federals in place at Washington. His plans were not proceeding as strategized.

Further, President Lincoln wanted Lee's army, badly. Lincoln gave a direct command to the Federal commander. No questions accepted: *"Lee's army, not Richmond, is your sure objective."*[4] From late June onward Robert E. Lee waned in ability to size up situations clearly. Increasingly he was discomfited, peaking in the three-day accidental battle at Gettysburg.

Virginia's General Lee expected pressure, of course. However, it escalated, piled up and dumped on him, as he lacked critical facts with which to make decisions—information such as the units of the Federal army, its direction, its size.

Lee's secret plan would have to be revised if it were to be accomplished. His revised task was to determine how to prepare for battle and yet bypass a general battle, in order to fulfill his secret deed.

The task bordered on the improbable.

And what George Gordon Meade would do, Lee couldn't surmise. He didn't know Meade's recent accomplishments or failures. Being on the move, Lee was devoid of up-to-date information about Meade.

The most immediate consideration was Meade's unknown location. Lee had not kept in touch with units in the rear of his own army, thinking Virginia was safe because of his recent Chancellorsville victory. Also, he had no knowledge of Meade's resources. Was the manpower of the Northern army greater or lesser than it had been at Chancellorsville?

Most importantly, Robert Lee didn't know whether or not Meade would fight. Would Meade be circumspect, maybe fearful, and simply try to contain the Victor of Chancellorsville? Was Meade's intent to steer his Southern army farther away from Washington, even marshal it back south into Virginia?

Lee's plans had called for the Army of Northern Virginia to go eastward, not to Gettysburg, but elsewhere. It is true that, "Lee intended to reunite his army near Gettysburg"[5] as Pulitzer Prize historian James M. McPherson notes, but there isn't an indication *from that time* that Lee intended to do battle there. "Prior to the battle this little town had no more importance than a point on a map where many roads happened to intersect."[6] Gettysburg was a way station to someplace else. It would accidentally become something else.

General Lee didn't tell any subordinate exactly where the army was headed; no longer did he have a "Stonewall" Jackson with whom he could plan unconventional actions. His cavalry commander, Stuart, "had expected to join up with Lee's infantry advance near York."[7] The secretive R. E. Lee had not told the plan *in toto* to Stuart. Nor to anyone, as far as is known. The *surpassing* raid was going somewhere else; troops as well as officers could only guess where.

Simply stated, the Confederate army was going someplace unheralded. It was going to York, the easternmost of the three counties in the soft underbelly of the Union. On the way, at the end of June, a division of General Richard Ewell's Second Corps captured Gettysburg and demanded money and supplies. Tradespeople and farmers pleaded more poverty than they evidenced. General Early, commander of that division, accepted their wails of destitution, and marched his troops out of Gettysburg eastward to York. Jubal Early didn't report back, to either Ewell or Lee, that any such useful thing as a shoe factory was in Gettysburg—nor that shoes were available other than those on civilians' feet. There wasn't much about that dusty crossroads town to excite visitors, much less conquerors.

General Lee also pestered himself about his cavalry commander, Major General James Ewell Brown Stuart. Lee expected information from Stuart about the Northern army and its movements. No information came, though, from the only source Lee had thought he needed; he didn't seek it from any other of his cavalry units.

"Jeb" Stuart had been issued discretionary, even inconsistent, orders by Lee and led his three regiments of cavalrymen behind the Federal lines. They entered Maryland near Washington, then passed Baltimore, creating consternation in both places among the citizenry. Lee, discerning Stuart's distance from the main body of the army, also discerned something about himself: immense consternation. Stuart's silence reduced Lee's outlook from active measures to cluelessness, approaching suspended animation. He became a human question mark. Comrades in arms began to notice a changing Lee.

On his part, Stuart was oblivious, as only Stuart could be when making a show. He knew not what he was doing to his commander in mind and in body. Lee needed information, gobs of it, in fact— particulars that cavalry could gather quickly. But, then, Stuart and his cavalrymen were eastward, beyond the Federal army where there wasn't much Federal activity; there wouldn't be pertinent information to pass on to Lee.

Stuart? Collecting booty and wagons—a hundred plus. He wanted to present prizes of supplies to General Lee.

Also, he fought a flashy skirmish with Federal cavalry at Hanover in York County which did not prove critical to either side. Eventually Stuart realized he had to obey orders, so he withdrew and headed to York. He accomplished one thing: Northerners knew—like famous "Kilroy was here" —that "Stuart was here." As per usual, he thought it was with dash. Everyone else thought it was rash.

Southern spies were not operative in York County where Lee's army was headed, nor were captured Union soldiers available to interrogate. Lee—without Stuart, spies, or squealers—needed so much more than he had. His plan was being compressed, boxed in. And compromised.

The General Commanding was blind without on-the-ground facts, particular items necessary to make decisions. "Distressed" may be too soft a word to describe R. E. Lee's mental condition as he attempted to formulate a strategy to meet Meade's Union army. "Horrified" may better describe his state of mind; scholars agree the distress affected him physically. Major G. Campbell Brown, staff officer and stepson of General Richard Ewell commander of the Second Corps, wrote crisply, contending Lee at Gettysburg was consumed by a "peculiar searching almost querulous impatience" and was "weak and in pain … suffering a great deal from diarrhea."[8]

Robert E. Lee didn't help himself, either.

He had sufficient cavalry units available; they could have been used for gathering information. In Lee's ranks were the Sixth, Seventh, Eleventh, and Thirty-fifth cavalry regiments from Virginia, as well as the two regiments Stuart had left behind in Virginia to guard the rear of the main army at the passes in the Blue Ridge hill country.[9]

Also available was Brigadier John Imbolden's cavalry division, not highly skilled, but experienced as irregulars on search-and-destroy missions. Still, Imbolden's division was cavalry and could have ranged over Adams and York counties for Lee. Imbolden's area of operation had *nothing* happening in it, in the mountains west and north of Chambersburg. Lee's failure to use his available cavalry resources for gathering information causes one to question whether or not the General remembered they were in his ranks! He was fixated on Stuart. Lee's grasp was loosening even before the battle at Gettysburg.

As he moved his troops eastward from Chambersburg and those at Greenwood Furnace still farther east on the Gettysburg Pike, Lee again didn't serve himself well. On the first day of the battle he confusedly ordered seven of his nine divisions up and over South Mountain at one time, on one road. The upshot was a logjam of considerable proportion; a snafu before the word was invented. It was a re-run of his failed campaign of 1861 in the Cheat Mountain area of northwestern Virginia. "Lee attempted to converge too many independent columns on the enemy position. The scheme failed," as J.T. Glathaar certified in *Partners In Command* (Free Press, 1994). He even used the same Pike for a critical period of ten hours to elbow through the wagon train of the Second Corps. Lee apparently was disorientated. Probably a greater problem, he was disorientating others.

Lee's errors, for a trained military engineer, were in no way defensible. An aftereffect caused some units, over a period of two days, to arrive late at the battlefield. What had he been thinking? A better question is: *How* had he been thinking? What mental processes had been operative? Or not operative? What emotional processes had occupied his mind instead of careful, cautious reasoning?

The upshot simply is that R. E. Lee didn't have his act together sufficiently to utilize his army efficiently.

Something was askew in his decision-making after he heard the news of the Federal Army of the Potomac's pursuit and George

Meade's presence. And then, when it came to the actual combat, Lee's discretionary orders at Gettysburg—which "Stonewall" would have been able to execute knowledgeably and readily—lay poorly executed when not delayed disturbingly. And he didn't know what the problem was.

A prime example of misunderstood discretionary order was given to Second Corps Commander General Ewell on the *first* day of fighting. Cemetery Hill should have been assaulted to finish the rout and flight of the Federal Army through Gettysburg, but Lee stated the order could be executed "*if* practicable." As commander, he allowed for non-adherence, non-compliance! He didn't grasp the situation firmly nor foresee its outcome distinctly. Lee needed "Chancellorsville Lee" at Gettysburg.

The ANV, consequently, never had an advantageous position that was close enough to pound the Union line. Had Ewell attacked on the *first* day—and succeeded—that late afternoon and early evening there wouldn't have been a hook in the fish-hook line of defense the Army of the Potomac had laid out so formidably.

Another plain fact became huge on the *second* day of the battle. It ruined Robert E. Lee's effort before he aggravated himself colossally the *third* day in the infamous Charge to the clump of trees at the stonewalled Angle. He could not—or *willfully* would not—see the obvious: geography!

"[T]he geographical influence in the wars." [10] Lee had researched the topic on his own volition when Superintendent at West Point. He seems to have remembered its importance the first day of battle though he didn't demand its application. And he seems to have forgotten it the second and third days. The man who had tamed the Mississippi River at St. Louis as a U.S. Army engineer, the man who had repaired forts up north and down south before the war, couldn't, or *wouldn't,* see the outright significance of the geography of the two Round Top hills south of the Union line.

Too late Lee must have understood General Longstreet's reluctance to make an open field uphill assault on the clump of trees at the Angle. As well, he must have understood the necessity to attain a higher place than the enemy's high place. The Round Top hills—Little and Big they came to be called—should have been seized early on, but Lee didn't note their significance soon enough, if at all.

Not notice heights? On the first day of the battle at Cemetery Hill on the northern section of the Federal line, he had rightly discerned their value. Why had he not recognized the out-and-out importance of even higher hills on the second day? They were visible, decidedly visible. Hugely visible in fact. Lee didn't see for looking!

Surely Lee had to be in pain for missing such important features. He should have been in pain for the bloodshed he was causing. He missed the obvious. He missed the fact that what was before his very eyes was more important than what was planned in his head.

Lee gave discretionary orders for the *third* day to the First Corps commander, General Longstreet, to begin his assault on the clump of trees across farmland almost a mile wide. Longstreet believed the frontal assault on the Federals was hopeless with their superior high ground advantage. True, Longstreet delayed implementing the fierce order, waiting until all his forces caught up with his units soon to be attacking. In the intervening time Federals placed men of iron will behind some stone walls and hillocks and in swales and grain fields to the left and right of the Angle where the Northern commander General Meade *knew* Lee would attack.

Having tried and failed on his left flank the *first* day and having tried and failed on his right flank the *second* day, Lee played the role of traditional *Northern* general and did the expected on the *third* day. He attacked the Union center.

Meade knew it. Bluecoats bided their time. The Union was in suspense.Lee's genius was gone. And it wasn't buried back in Virginia alongside dead "Stonewall" Jackson. It was buried in his own head beneath a plan for peace, which expired among the orchards and fields, boulders and blunders of the Gettysburg battlefield.

The wall of that crucial Angle was close to three feet high. That height, added to the uphill approach, made the Angle area a mini-fortress that would have to be seized by soldiers one-by-one-by-one, since units would be jammed against the wall, waiting to climb or crawl over it uphill. They wouldn't be able to vault uphill over the wall; they weren't Olympic champions.

Utter bravery would be necessary man-by-man-by-man. But even utter bravery in a stupid action doesn't assure success. All their valor would meet Bluecoats face-to-face-to-face, Northern men whose equal valor was magnified on their own soil and directed by a strategy to knock out a knockout blow.

Bluecoated Yanks, stacked tightly together behind the wall, aimed firearms straight at clambering, scrambling Graycoats with heads exposed, hearts bared, guts uncovered, too. It was a terrifying nightmare for the men, as they had marched through open fields under cannon fire, climbed over split-rail fences with added rifle fire, and crossed a clear road to get at Yanks so like themselves, while being attacked from both sides as well as the front. Hell comes at a warrior from all around.

Yet that horrible prospect and the reality of it were both met with Southern courage, albeit a kind of daring not wise. Not really. A few would succeed against shell and shot. More would die climbing.

The few, the 150 or so Confederates who succeeded, failed. Capture would have been a blessing contrasted with the many who met lethal reapers from the front, the left, the right. The Last Reaper at the wall of the Angle slashed through faces and chests and loins. Quick deaths ended long dreams of independence, and contorted with grief the lives of loved ones back home. Thus ended belief in a Lord of Hosts siding where human minds can never really discern. So very much died at that Angle.

None, not one on that rampart turned tail, whether gray or blue coated. Union troops at the Angle were in a thin line of defenders; they were fewer in number than the men who succeeded in climbing over the wall only to fail. Brave, brave defenders and six supposedly silenced cannons made the difference.[11]

The Southern delay by discretionary order before the ill-conceived Charge gave Meade time to device a tactic that would surprise—and decimate—the so-called Pickett's Charge. Federal artillery would cannonade for a specific length of time, then seemingly die out, cannon by cannon, as they purposely ceased firing. That action of inaction would give the appearance that Federal artillery at the Angle—the focus of the Confederate charge on the third day— was destroyed or was fleeing bombardment.

The tactic worked; the planned silence heartened Confederate forces. Through the battlefield smoke it looked to them as if the remaining Federal artillery pieces were hightailing it out of the battle. Smoggy air provided the North a successful ruse.

The Rebels were mystified by the "destroyed" artillery. Such a Northern tactic was made possible because Southern delay eroded Southern good sense. Lee was right—vinegary cruel—Meade would make no blunder in front of him, and if he blundered Meade would surely take advantage of it. Advantage: George G. Meade.

The Union "silenced" batteries were unsilenced. Canister and grapeshot mowed down scores of Johnny Rebs just when they thought they were *not* going to be hectored by cannon shot and shell, musket balls and rifle bullets. From the front, from the right, from the left, the charging assault was in turn assaulted by troops embedded in their native soil.

Lee had used only eleven of his thirty-eight infantry brigades in the assault. Out in the open he was attempting to split the entrenched Army of the Potomac with less than a third of his own army. A majority watched in horror from the Secessionist side as their comrades-in-arms were split off from the land of the living.

The faulty charge failed; the battle failed; hope began to fail. Finally, in less than two more years, everything failed.

The post-Charge situation was mournful. Lee admitted it was all his fault. It was. He had disdained too long the soldiers' hypothesis: Offense wins acclaim, but defense, more often, wins battles. His previously bravado words to Longstreet, "If the enemy is there in the morning, we *must* attack him," turned to blood, guts, death, defeat; his admission of error properly placed in the Losers' Dustbin of history.

Wretchedly, one of Lee's prior decisions had come back to obliterate good men in the assault. That choice certainly had to have loaded the General with guilt. If he did not feel guilty he was not human. He had to have remembered cutting off his supply line eight days before the bloody charge, thereby denying troops adequate protection by artillery to have truly softened up the Federals. His men were hurt badly, died needlessly.

Self-reproach: Lee's ammunition for artillery had run low, terribly low. The closest ammunition depot was 150 miles south in Dixie—in the Shenandoah Valley at Staunton, Virginia. Yet he used up most of his supply. "Hill's artillery was wasting much of its scanty ammunition."[12] Colonel E. P. Alexander, whom Lieutenant General James Longstreet tried to co-opt to order General George Pickett to begin the disastrous Charge to the Angle, wrote, "If, as I infer from your note, there is an alternative to this attack, it should be carefully considered before opening our fire, for it will take all the artillery ammunition we have left, and if the result is unfavorable we will have none left for another effort. And even if this [attack] is entirely successful, it can be so only at a very bloody cost."[13]

The Lee worshipper, Douglas Freeman, summed up the woeful situation that his idol, R. E. Lee, had caused: "The greater part of the artillery was almost *powerless* for lack of ammunition."[14]

The words of the Confederate Chief of Ordnance, Josiah Gorgias, about Lee's felt necessity to capture Winchester, Virginia two weeks before the Gettysburg phase of the Northern campaign, pertain precisely to Lee's cutting off his supply line a week later: "What this movement means is difficult to divine." Isn't cutting off one's own supply line when invading enemy territory tantamount to destroying one's army, no matter what reason is behind it? Isn't it grounds for a court martial?

Repeatedly it is said about R. E. Lee concerning the battle of Gettysburg in general or the Charge to the Angle on the third day that "his blood was up" and that he wanted a decisive battle. He had laid bare his hand on the first day by assaulting the right wing of the Union line and then the second day by assaulting his enemy's left wing. Any newly scrubbed lieutenant could tell where he would at-tack the third: the center.

Lee's blood may have been up but it wasn't feeding his brain. Something paralyzed his engineer's analytical mind: his imposing plan had indeed decomposed before the horrific retreat from the Angle.

The kindest interpretation of Lee's situation is that the Gettysburg landscape of verdant fields, graceful woods, blooming flowers, time-sculpted boulders, and forested hills had become a wilderness of confusion. It was R. E. Lee's personal wasteland.

People around the General witnessed something about him for at least five days prior, starting 28 June, to 3 July in the Gettysburg phase of the Pennsylvania Campaign; something they had not beheld at its beginning nor in its retreat phase. The Leeophile Freeman, in his twentieth-century four-volume interpretation of Lee, had to deal with that difference in order to be truthful and respectable as a biographer:

> Captain Justus Scheibert, the Prussian [official military] ob-server, who had been with Lee at Chancellorsville and had noticed his quiet demeanor on that field, remarked after the war that "in the days of Gettysburg his quiet self-possessed calmness was wanting." Lee, he said, "was not at ease, but was riding to and fro, frequently changing his position, mak-ing anxious inquiries here and there, and looking *careworn*."[15]

And Professor James Robertson, the contemporary scholar in America who teaches the consistently largest-attended courses on the "Civil War Era" and charter member of the Virginia Civil War Sesquicentennial (150th anniversary) Commission, crisply notes the whole story: "Lee was not in good health at Gettysburg." No ques-tion; Lee was sick. Lee was *careworn*.

No wonder Major G. Campbell Brown observed that Lee at Gettysburg was consumed by a "peculiar searching almost querulous impatience" and was "weak and in pain—suffering a great deal from diarrhea."[16]

That bout of poor health of the Southern chieftain is often blamed on superfluous matters, and is said to have lasted only on the second day of the battle. Supposedly the black raspberries Lee loved so much made him ill. He received some berries from a boy, Leighton Parks—the same lad he had met upon entering Maryland in the earlier campaign of September 1862, a campaign that ended in the bloodiest *day* of the whole war. In 1863 Lee would have eaten the berries a week or so before 2 July, and before the three-day bloodiest *battle* of the war. Yet black raspberries were not likely to cause diarrhea so long and late after eating them.

The same thing happened when he crossed the Mason-Dixon Line into Pennsylvania. Another person gifted him with black raspberries: a Pennsylvania Dutch *hausfrau*. She presented a "mess"—as they call it—of them to the invader. This view is also out of touch with reality because the gifting took place not quite a week before 2 July, the fancied single day of ill health, again long before diarrhea happened. A physical tidbit needs mentioning at this point: black raspberries can cause constipation, diarrhea is not likely.

When the black raspberry calculation misfired, exponents of the superfluous ascribed cherries as culprits for his diarrhea. However, there isn't documentation for such similar gifting events as exist about the Maryland lad and the Pennsylvania housewife. And R. E. Lee was not a petty thief: he didn't pilfer them riding under cherry trees.

A compelling precious particle of historical gold about Lee's ill health did come down to us from an astute observer, a physician. It occurred Monday, 29 June 1863, the morning *after* Lee had heard the spy's report at ten o'clock Sunday night, 28 June. That news shattered more than the quiet time following Sunday evening vesper services in camp.

The Sunday evening news we know; it was was bad, disruptively bad: George Gordon Meade was the new commander of the Federal army. General Meade was in the field. The Army of the Potomac was not back defending Washington!

The Monday morning news is comparatively new to us. General

Lee was sick; *careworn* sick, disruptively sick, *days before* battle erupted at Gettysburg as his men shot first contrary to his orders.

Lee was apprehensive. It extended to physical agony It surely impressed Dr. J. L. Suesserott, one of Chambersburg's leading physicians, although the doctor did not understand its cause. He visited Lee on Monday, June 29, to obtain an exemption of his neighbor's blind mare from seizure by the Confederates.

While General Lee had the paper prepared, the physician studied the features and movements of the noted commander. He said he *had never seen so much emotion* depicted on a human countenance as on Lee's. "With his hands at time clutching his hair, and with contracted brow, he would walk with rapid strides for a few rods and then, as if he bethought himself of his actions, he would *with a sudden jerk* produce an *entire change* in his features and demeanor and cast an inquiring gaze on me, only to be followed in a moment by the same contortions of face and agitation of person."[17] Even if allowance is made for subjective evaluation it is clear that Lee was *deeply disturbed* or *physically unwell*.

Clearly Robert Edward Lee had been suffering earlier than 2 July. Though some of his physical condition may have related to eating certain foods, more than likely much was related to facts-on-the-ground. Psychological disruptions often result in physical eruptions. And Robert Lee was a psychological case before the battle.

Meade's presence had messed up Lee's plans for the Northern Campaign. Lee couldn't help but be disturbed *deeply*. Deep intrusions certainly can cause deep psychological devastations.

Lee would have been shocked by the news, or fearful, at worst. He would have feared losing. He would have feared losing an opportunity for peace. He would have feared losing everything. Lee was in a psychosomatic condition, ailing. Traumatized relentlessly.

Questions undoubtedly would have arisen in a rational man's mind. How can I accomplish my plan? What will happen to my proposal of peace? What will happen to my plan "not to bring on a general battle" while up North? What would happen if— contrary to orders—my troops shot first?

R. E. Lee paid a mental price, from 29 June 1863 onward. He paid a price, physically, as well.

Sick for days, Lee was off balance bodily, emotionally, intellectually. It would be more accurate, certainly more considerate, to say he was sick at heart—essentially sick to the center of his being. Buttermilk had been his life-long self-prescribed remedy when ill. But buttermilk couldn't reach the depth of *"deeply disturbed."*

Then misjudgments arose, passively at first.

Next occurred miscues, errors, lapses, misunderstandings, missed opportunities on the battlefield for three days in July—before a Fourth of July celebration and peace proclamation could ever be presented at York.

Havoc followed: "If Lee falls back again, it will be the darkest day for the Confederacy we have yet seen."[18] Darkness fell. It overlay every Confederate military action thereafter.

Lee, affirmed his most prominent biographer, Freeman, was "wrecked at Gettysburg."[19]

Chapter Notes

1. Douglas Southall Freeman. R.E.Lee: A Biography (N.Y.: Scribner's, 1934): Vol. III. 150.
2. Ibid. III. 153.
3. Edwin B. Coddington. The Gettysburg Campaign: A Study in Command (N.Y.: Touchstone/Simon and Schuster, 1968): 196.
4. WR/OR. I. 27. 1. 35.
5. James M. McPherson. Battle Cry of Freedom: The Civil War Era (N.Y.: Ballantine, 1989): 653.
6. Coddington, The Gettysburg Campaign.128.
7. Thomas L. Connelly. The Marble Man: Robert E. Lee and His Image in American Society (N.Y.: Knopf, 1977): 88.
8. W. W. Blackford. War Years With Jeb Stuart (N.Y.: Scribner's, 1945): 230-31.
9. E. H. Bonekemper III. How Robert E. Lee Lost The Civil War (Spotsylvania, Va: Kirkland's Press, 1999): 108, Note 26.

10. Elizabeth Brown Pryor, Reading The Man. (N.Y.: Viking, 2007.): 220.

11. Coddington. The Gettysburg Campaign. 796-97. Note 97.

12. Freeman. Lee. III. 111.

13. Ibid. 115-16.

14. Ibid. 133. (Emphasis added)

15. Freeman. Lee. III. 90.

16. W. W. War Years With Jeb Stuart (N.Y.: Scribner's. 1945): 230-31.

17. Glen Tucker. High Tide At Gettysburg (Indianapolis: Bobbs-Merrill, 1958): 88.

18. John B. Jones. A Rebel War Clerk's Diary (Phila.: Lippincott, 1866): Vol. I. 374.

19. Douglas Southall Freeman. Unpublished Letters of General Rober E. Lee, C.S.A. to Jefferson Davis and the War Department of the Confederate States of America 1862-1865. Revised Edition. (N.Y.: Putnam's, 1957): xxxvii.

CHAPTER **21**

Undoomed Warrior

FROM THE TIME he was a boy Robert E. Lee lived in a shadow.

The shadow first took shape when his father deserted the family leaving him without a direct male influence, a father figure. His role model at age five—if he had one—would have had to be abstract. He had little education at that point in his life to have known or heard of a real one, except for George Washington. But dead President Washington was not physically real to him while a Washington-in-the-head was not a comfort on cold winter nights, nor a trailblazer in the daylight. And, certainly, the Father of our Country was not a help to Robert's sickly mother.

The boy's shadowy existence could have darkened into the forlorn gloom of a n'er-do-well or the cramped selfishness of a lone wolf. The young R. E. Lee could have grown to hate his father, Henry "Lighthorse Harry" Lee, who deserted family and country.

The boy become a lad, Robert Lee had to fill adult shoes, do adult work, and extend adult care to his convalescent mother with little time for usual childhood antics or adolescent excitements. He could have been doomed to oblivion, or been beclouded by obscurity a few years after his birth and into adulthood.

It was as if a dismal overcast of emotional thunderheads or dust storms tracked him. To say he was manly—his own man, at such an early age—is to impute American optimism where it doesn't fit. Notwithstanding, the worst conditions of young life, early death or forced obscurity, never befell him as he grew through boyhood into budding young adulthood. He survived; he must have held firm to something. Or to Someone. His destiny was other than demise or oblivion, though the destiny he craved never came to be.

In his early forties the shadow over Lee lengthened and turned into a phantasmagoria. With hair-raising intensity and searing physical proximity it confronted him with his own death. The danger was so stark that afterward one would imagine he would have had jet-black night-terrors emerge violently, attacking him in bright day as during the burnt umber of sleep or the reddish aggresion of sleeplessness.

Lee didn't dwell on the shadowy ordeal. Perhaps the reason for his seldom mentioning the event is that it didn't happened on the massive killing fields of the "great civil war" that President Abraham Lincoln addressed sixteen years later in Gettysburg.

But the event had overtaken him in a war—in the American war before the "civil" one. The young Lincoln had strongly opposed that war, a criticism that cost him his re-election bid for the Congressional House of Representatives. War costs are varied in terms of death and destruction, on friend and foe alike. Everyone is scathed.

The Mexican-America conflict had been a war of choice. But multitudes of Americans openly and broadly opposed the choice of war with Mexico. Others saw wealth and new lands. Discord was rampant across America.

Former President John Quincy Adams viewed the war as a naked land-grab by America. Dauntlessly, on the floor of Congress, he proclaimed the war to be evil.

The war with Mexico was so bad that later President Ulysses S. Grant, a lieutenant brevetted two times during that war, wrote in his *Personal Memoirs*, "to this day I regard the war … as one of the most unjust wars ever waged by a stronger against a weaker nation. It was an instance of a republic following the bad example of European monarchies in not considering justice in their desire to acquire additional territory."[1] Bad wars are "badder" when good nations initiate them; they have the "baddest" consequences.

The popular name for the conflict was "Mr. Polk's War." It was a war that President James Polk glamorized as a way to expand the nation westward to California and southwestward to Texas. Supposedly those lands were part of America's "Manifest Destiny" to fill the continent.

Manifest Destiny was a fiction, a political fiction concocted to give Americans a goal, a new frontier. No other nation accepted the fiction as fact.

R. E. Lee served in the war that resulted from such brashness. The War with Mexico, 1846-48, was an adventure for him, exciting. He grew in wisdom and strength and in favor with his commander and fellow officers. Courageous and skillful, he was always in good report with Commanding General Winfield Scott. Scott's high estimation of Lee continued throughout the general's life, present even fourteen years later when Lee rejected his oath as an officer of the United States Army, resigning to serve another master.

In the course of the American invasion of Mexico, Lee faced something about himself that only grew clearer with time; he was not doomed to die an early death nor to die in war. That condition surfaced again six years later at the death of his decidedly impressive mother-in-law, Mary Fitzhugh Custis. He was affected with more than sadness at her death; he loved her as he had loved his own mother. Ten years later the condition resurfaced again at the death of his military alter ego, Thomas J. Jackson, called "Stonewall." And then another seven years later it emerged in a strange but marvelous way while vacationing with a daughter, a few months before his death.

That frightful event during the Mexican War was reported by the most intellectual of American military officers, called "The Pen of the Army," Ethan Allen Hitchcock, grandson of the Revolutionary War hero Ethan Allen. When Commandant at Corpus Christi the later-to-be Major General Hitchcock wrote in his diary on 20 March 1847:

Capt. R. E. Lee, one of the engineers and an admirable officer, had a narrow escape with his life yesterday. Returning from a working party with Lieut. P. T. Beauregard, he turned a point in the path in the bushes and suddenly came up on one of our soldiers who no doubt mistook him for a Mexican and challenged "Who goes there?" "Friend" said Captain Lee. "Officers" said Beauregard at the same time, but the soldier in trepidation and haste leveled a pistol at Lee and fired. The ball passed between his left arm and body—the flame singeing his coat because he was so near.[2]

Evaluating that event took the adult Robert Edward Lee back to the times as a boy his famous father, Henry "Light-Horse Harry" Lee, had shared his Deist religious values with his family. One of those values came into action after the shooting: Captain Lee did not want the soldier punished. His commander was abashed.

Simply put, Captain Lee understood that "things happen," meaning accidents do happen in the Universe and no one is rationally responsible. Deists contend God had created the world and imprinted it with laws to run on its own without godly intervention. Thus, things happen outside God's purview, range of authority or control, things not ordered by God. Some happenings are unfortunate and no one knows the reason(s) nor the law(s), if there are any, behind the happenings. Sometimes decent human beings are involved unexpectedly in terrible situations and cannot, in all fairness, be blamed for their actions or inactions. Things happen. Period. That's the way it is, no more no less. Sometimes there is no fault in human existence because there is no willful human cause. Exclamation point!

Captain Lee reacted calmly to the shooting event, expressing compassionate consideration for the soldier. His immediate superior would not hear of it. No one knows what self-assertive Beauregard thought.

Doubtless Lee felt something or he would not have intervened on the trooper's behalf. How could it be that he did not express negative emotion? Something way out of the ordinary had happened to him. Was he lucky? Then again, blessed wouldn't be an exaggeration, especially in a nasty war at a wretched place, for a cause dubious at best, wrong at worst. It was a terrorizing experience yet R. E. Lee "let it be."

Another explanation for some people was that Lee was saved by an act of grace from a loving God. Possibly. One can believe what one wishes; one cannot know for certain how an Infinite Being acts.

For some other people the incident was pure happenstance. A twist in time. A wrinkle in the fabric of space. Possibly. One can suppose what one wants; to know is not a certainty, often even for the human beings involved in events.

Or, others could interpret it as a portent of what's to come in life. Possibly. Even likely; various situations in life do repeat, repeat, and repeat, for unknown reasons.

Whatever the case, the incident was bewildering: Lee shot at close range, near the heart, still alive, unshaken. From appearances the situation and his undoomed condition sank into his subconscious mind. Until the next war.

Captain Lee briskly relied on what he knew best: duty. He returned to what he did best, military duty, and succeeded most creditably in Mexico.

Duty characterized Robert E. Lee, clear as the hair on his face. He was the personification of Aristotle's *Nicomachean Ethics* summed up as: We are what we do repeatedly. Excellence in life is not a single action but the habit of a lifetime.[3] Lee was duty personified—but living in a society-become-lackadaisical.

It became evident to R. E. Lee that the American Revolution for political freedom of the 1770s and '80s had passed away a generation or two previous. Revolutionary zest had waned. Things were transmuting. Change was in the air—air that oft times stank to high heaven with the rotting remnants of patriotism.

In the place of Revolutionary freedom, splits among Americans were unmasked. Economic outlooks, population constituencies, financial disparities and contrasting ideas about human servitude—namely slavery—were mixed, lumped together. Inextricably and without compromise these incompatible parts made up the American agglomeration.

The split over slavery carried the sharpest, meanest contrast between sections of the American Republic.

Some people were comfortable with the notion that certain people had the right to own other people as property no different from furniture or land or animals. The simple underlying reason for the split dealt with the concept that certain human beings are "property" because they are an inferior race. And that race is black.

At the founding of the American Republic the Southern states were granted an oddity—or two—about "human property." In the first instance the Constitution accepted that black people who were bought, or born, as property—that is, slaves—were recognized as a "states rights" issue of chattel, personal property, an issue the central government could not invalidate. In the second instance, the same Constitution Article I, Section 3 declared that "free persons, including those bound to service for a term of years and excluding Indians not taxed [and] three fifth of all other persons" were to be enumerated for election purposes, effectively classifying blacks as "three-fifths" persons.

Most Southerners were accepting of a political puzzle: blacks as human property or blacks as three-fifths human beings. Both parts of the quandary were physically, intellectually, and spiritually agreeable because their Bibles and wallets told them so.

Many people, as well, were oblivious to the notion of human property being a problem at all. Also three-fifths is not bad since 50/50 in an acquisitive society is always better than less, and three-fifths is even more than half! Like the poor, the oblivious are with us always.

Still others were vociferously opposed to the notion that living human beings can be owned in any way or manner.

Protection of property by the laws of the land composed the core of the resurgent sectionalism of North and South. Left over from the constitutional debates at the Republic's founding six decades earlier, Sectional North and Sectional South were at one anothers' throats.

Robert E. Lee was deeply disturbed by the differences held by members of the sections. He thought slavery would gradually disappear from America and so should not be disrupted in mid-nineteenth century America. As well, he thought slavery was more damaging to white people than black people, though there isn't any record that he consulted black people about that evaluation. But there were hot heads on each side of the slaves-as-property issue and property-as-a-states-rights issue. The matter would cause a revolution. Lee absolutely opposed revolution as unconstitutional, a view he expressed in a letter to his son Custis on 23 January 1861, three months prior to the war:

> Secession is nothing but revolution. The framers of our Constitution ... intended for perpetual union, so expressed in the preamble and for the establishment of a government, not a compact, which can only be dissolved by a revolution, or the consent of all the people in convention assembled.

Feeling "out of it" intellectually, emotionally and socially from the mid-1840s through the '50s into the early 1860s, R. E. Lee was dead-ended.

Mary Fitzhugh Custis, his mother-in-law, however was of kindlier outlook. She was, by nature, a remarkable person. Her faith was evangelical, unashamedly. Hers was a warm, glowing heart for her Lord and a just-as-warm helping hand for people. Belief and Relief were twins for Mother Molly. They were of one cloth, the same essence, a Christian "can't have one without the other." She was on top of her world with joy because of the love she had for God in response to the love she sensed flowing from God. She was the Christian Faith in a female body.

The home of Mary Fitzhugh Custis was one where another Mary—her sister Martha, too, of Bible fame—could have stepped in from another time, another place. In the Custis' home there was time to talk about noble things with a visiting master and at the same time do ordinary chores for others, cooking and serving, then washing a sink full of dishes for the next visitor. There wasn't a dichotomy of intellect and action, between faith and deed, in Mary Custis' home.

Boldly, for a woman of the South, Mary F. Custis had freed her slaves, in opposition to her husband who would not free his. She freed them as Another had freed the halt, the blind, the sick, the seekers of health and wholeness. All day, every day, she lived the Faith.

Mrs. Custis engulfed her live-in son-in-law, R. E. Lee, with care, with a joy that passed his understanding. In whatever way, her engulfment did not smother his appreciation for her. Robert Lee adored her, it seemed, as much as he had his own compassionate mother.

In 1853, Mary Fitzhugh Custis' death stunned Lee. It didn't just butt in on his life as death often does. It stunned. Her death mattered; it shattered the brave man.

At the time she died R. E. was in a bastion away from home. It was a bulwark made to protect. But West Point couldn't protect against the death of one deeply loved in its superintendent's life. With a poignancy fed by the deepest pathos, Lee wrote that it was "the most affecting calamity that has ever befallen us."[4]

Lee set out to be like her. He would walk in Mother Molly's footsteps.

A bit later he did walk, to her grave. At the dirt-filled site with a grass covering there "was a scene for pity to behold," a cousin wrote, "to see that strong man weep so bitterly," as he sobbed uncontrollably.[5]

Words may carry the highest tribute at the time of death but tears of grief are the deepest of tributes. Tears well up from a depth within us that we seldom admit to; they come from within solid flesh and solid bone, so close to the beating heart and the breathing lungs. They flow from a tactile body, bidding to anoint the precious body grown cold, now out of reach under earth. Tears are tangible things—not musings or ponderings of the mind about the mysteries of life and death, which wing briskly on to other thoughts. Tears wash away unbelief many a time.

Lee wept. Uncontrollably. Bitterly. And something happened.

At that grave he had an epiphany as he faced death. There he turned; there he faced *his* death. At Mother Molly's grave he knew that the bullet passing between thorax and arm in 1847 had not doomed him.

Worthy of attention and contemplation, death brings sorrow, of course, but many times it brings grace. At death, something is needed since sorrow depletes humanness. Grace fills that void and enhances humanness, deepens it. It did so in Lee's life.

Mother-in-law Mary Custis died 23 April 1853. Within three months Robert Edward Lee committed to Christianity. He was confirmed, "made firm," in Christ Episcopal Church, Alexandria, Virginia 17 July 1853.

An adult, forty-six years of age, Lee joined a church for the first time in his life—with his daughters Mary and Annie. Together they received the Sacrament of Holy Communion, the first public religious act in his life. His commitment to the Christian Faith confirmed, it became a prominent and daily experience. Molly Custis' faith became R. E. Lee's daily fare.

Up to his death at age sixty-three, the Faith was meaningful for Lee. For years he had presided as senior warden of the vestry of his home congregation, Grace Episcopal Church, Lexington, during his tenure as President of Washington College. In Autumn 1780, following a long vestry meeting he walked home afterwards in a drizzling rain not fully protected. Experiencing a chill, he took to his bed. Other maladies took over his body.

R. E. Lee died a man of Faith 12 October 1870, undoomed, moving forward.

Of course undoomed didn't mean he wouldn't die. Undoomed meant that nothing in life—expressly, nothing in his own life—ever would or could keep him from holding firm. It was his duty to hold firm in the Faith.

That undoomed nature had emerged in stages throughout in Robert Lee's life.

His father might *not* have deserted the family for the Caribbean and could have acculturated Bobbie into becoming a Virginia dandy. He then could reel around on a dance floor or ride herd on a field of slaves planting corn or cotton instead of leading an army of beloved and bedraggled soldiers and earning their acclaim.

Or he might *not* have attended the Military Academy and might have gone to Harvard College instead. Immersed in numerals, formulas, proofs and calculations as an academic pedagogue, he might not have been heard of again. He might have slipped into obscurity rather than rising as a leader who exemplified virtue and faithfulness to a strata of the human family.

Or he might *not* have become a small college president "in a place of no importance," as one of his former generals said, rather than serving as an example of the educated Christian gentleman which he saw as *the* goal for each and every Washington College student.

Or he might *not* have become a man of principle who accepted black Americans as human beings—albeit not capable of intelligent voting—but rather might have become a plantation owner at Arlington, justifying slavery to maintain a cavalier lifestyle of ease, alcohol, hunting, family, and gossip, always gossip.

Or he might *not* have been true to his arthritic wife and seven children—more than half his married life he was away from his family on military duty—rather than easily dallying with women from New York to Texas where no one would know, or care.

Or he might *not* have been an educator preparing young men for life in a changed re-United States of America, rather than becoming a radical Secessionist who after the war could have been chief of guerilla fighters or of white-hooded night-riders promoting white supremacy.

Or he might *not* have been a leader of a decidedly impoverished and hidden rural college that quickly became an innovative school which grew into an excellent university, free of sectarian or political control rather than an insurance company shill, as offered to him, earning $10,000 to 50,000 a year for the commercial use of his name.

Or he might *not* have become an eminent American having more books written about him than any other American except Abraham

Lincoln, rather than becoming an engineer after West Point constructing buildings or laying out drain fields.

Or he *might* have accepted the position as Commanding General of the Federal army at the beginning of the war in 1861, changing American history. Then his statue as *victor* at some-other-Gettysburg would be placed off to the side of some-other-Hancock Avenue where hardly anyone would visit or care about it—as happened to Major General George Gordon Meade, victor of the actual battle at Gettysburg! Adding insult to injury, the victor's statue would again not be listed on the National Park Service map "Touring the Battlefield" for all not to recognize.

All the while, the monument for the *loser* of that some-other-Gettysburg battle would be prominently situated with extensive grounds, drive-around road, and parking area for visitors to view the ignominious yet famous field where brave men were senselessly slaughtered by order of a sick commander. American history would be changed thoroughly.

Or, he might have *ended* his own life! Early on the day of his surrender at Appomattox 9 April 1865 he revealed a side of himself not even imagined by his dearest friends. It must have been a side of himself with which he wrestled after the defeat at Gettysburg, when he sought to resign from his position. Jefferson Davis would not allow that resignation because it would have been a propaganda blow at the heart of the Confederacy, one that the North would have manipulated successfully. Lee may have experienced the same emotional hell after the Antietam retreat in '62 and followed by various defeats in 1864-65 of the war. He was a wrestler with death.

The immense pressure upon him as a battlefield commander surveying masses and multitudes, heaps and piles of dedicated and loyal, courageous and starving men who died, serving under him, eventually got to R. E. Lee. He told his staff, "How easily I could get rid of all this and be at rest! I have only to ride along the lines and all will be over!" Like Socrates and Jesus he might have allowed others to end his life. His anguish was that of a sensitive soul—not a remorseful loser. "But it is our duty to live."[6]

Life's choices come at us formidably. Often it feels as if Life will wither us with one blast of truth, harshly driving us to pick a side. "Once to every man and nation comes the moment to decide," wrote James Russell Lowell, "And the choice goes by forever 'twixt that darkness and that light."

Every human life is unique, of course in some way. R. E. Lee's destiny was so precisely unique that it's difficult to believe it happened as it did. Every major step could have lead to obscurity, or early death at various junctions if it had been lived otherwise. He might even have been undoomed, so unique was he, but it would have been in a different way with a different panache.

Lee's was not a charmed life magically protected, not one better than other persons' lives, however. It was a life lived dutifully causing him to stand above most everyone, even some of the other great human beings throughout history.

Logical engineer, rational leader—and a dearly loved leader of men—he realized his undoomed life was beyond wizardry and without religious adornment of any sort. He accepted, modestly, that spiritual peace sheltered him. Daily prayer engendered strength in Robert Edward Lee as he sought the Socratic virtue: *gnothi se sauton,* *"Know thyself."*

His life, accordingly, was lived as a *duty* to himself, *duty* to others, *duty* to family, *duty* to homeland, *duty* to God. In time, all that was *duty*, or *duties*, would not so much save R. E. Lee as direct his pathways. In spite of victories or defeats—any victories or many retreats—he was fulfilling his life in obedience. He moved in obedience to some inner light that shone a way—blurred, but nonetheless away from war and towards a possible reconciliation within himself, with his family, with his dead comrades, with a new beginning for young men, Virginia, and the nation.

ر.ر.ر.

Of course there were critics who castigated R. E. Lee. There still are. Why should there not be? Greatness is so sweeping, so grand, that it can't help but attract opposition. There is so much in great men and women that it's too much for some people to stomach.

Critics of great men and great women often use the simile of clay feet, citing an idiom "our idols have clay feet." They imply the great ones among us necessarily have faulty underpinnings, foundations that *definitely* will crumble much as clay objects are short-lived, and deteriorate because the on-ground part invariably falls apart.

Regardless of how some critics look at great people, the historical image of clay feet doesn't point necessarily to such fragility or deficiency. Rather,

> This image, mighty and of exceeding brightness, has an appearance that is frightening. The head of the image is of fine gold, its breast and arms of silver, its belly and thighs of bronze, its legs of iron, and its feet *partly* of iron and *partly* of clay. ... [T]he feet and the toes are *partly* of potter's clay and *partly* of iron it shall be divided but some of the firmness of iron shall be in it ... so it shall be *partly* strong and *partly* weak.[7]

Lee, even before religion became integral to his life, never denied that he was an admixture of strength and weakness, of good and evil, *"partly of iron and partly of clay,"* if you will. He did not say he could not fail.

He made it his duty, however, to prepare as fully as possible not to fail. Certainly not to fail as a husband as had his father. Certainly not as an engineer; he aimed to be as precise as a mathematician. He desired to be a proper soldier on parade ground or battle ground—disciplined and dedicated. Nor did he want to fail as a leader of men whose very lives were in his heart as much as his head, when he would take them into battle. Lee made it his duty not to fail. Not to fail himself. Or others.

We can say factually R. E. Lee's "feet" were partly iron, partly clay. Nonetheless he prepared his life and actions in such fashion that the admixture of purposes and preparations, means and ends, would not *have* to crumble. He disciplined himself that he would not fall apart in ordinary, matter of course events, nor under pressure from external events. He was self-governing to the extent that even his bad temper did not destroy others, as he would voluntarily relent in some way after he exploded. True, he seldom apologized when in error, yet he appeared not to carry a grudge into the future. Except there was a huge grudge he had against his slaves from his father-in-law's estate, whom he had to free by that relative's will, but Lee did not do so until under court order, and then only on last day of that order! Lee suffered the human failure of racism concerning black people, not endemic to the South alone but the North too, the planet also. Racism is an attack upon humanness based on pigment not principle, color not character.

Lee did not make public display of his shortcomings; it was not in his personality to do so. And just as honestly, he did not publicly announce his *virtus*, his power, manly excellence, abilities, strengths. It was not in his personality to do so. Definitely it was not in him to be gaudy or tasteless, ever.

The proper gentleman that was R. E. Lee saw his public duty as duty *not* to make himself the center of Confederate policy or the Confederate war effort. The Pennsylvania Campaign, for example, was manifestly his plan yet at first appeared to be government strategy, especially after four days of planning with the top officials, 14 - 17 May 1863.

That appearance of government management of the Campaign may have been the very reason he was not provided what he thought fit for his unique plan. Government rationale that there was a "Lee advantage" could have been the reason he couldn't get the troops he thought necessary for the action in the North. There is a possibility the "Lee advantage" was the reason his request for a fake army, an army in effigy to pin down the Union army to defend Washington, D.C., was rejected.

Lee in early battles had had Lee on his side! An incalculable value, to be sure.

The mystique of a supreme strategist and tactician rolled into one helped him out-general opponents. No wonder he thought that under the right circumstance he had an invincible army, if only he had the right officers. Confederate officialdom, like the public, sometimes thought Lee invincible under *every* circumstance.

Too may assumed General Lee had such a negative effect on Yankee military officials that his reputation alone could replace troops. Some thought—irrationally—that his fearsome reputation among ordinary Bluecoats was worth another division, making Lee worth two divisions in the field! It's easy to forget that success can lead to failure. Or—as jaws drop—that success can itself be a failure! Triumph in what is the comparatively short time of a battle can result in believing a whole war is also won in an instance. A disastrous belief, for sure.

During the Pennsylvania Campaign of 1863 Lee could have used those two make-believe divisions which some thought he was worth. His plan failed at Gettysburg. Two divisions times two wouldn't have helped because his plan *not* to have a general battle, unless attacked, was broken by his own men:

Report of Capt. J. J. Young, quartermaster Twenty-sixth North Carolina Infantry

> Near Gettysburg, Pa.
> *July 4, 1863.*

My Dear Governor: I will trespass a few minutes upon your indulgence to communicate the sad fate that has befallen the old Twenty-sixth. The heaviest conflict of the war has taken place in this vicinity. It commenced July 1, and raged furiously until late last night. Heth's Division, of A. P. Hill's Corps *opened the ball*, and Pettigrew's brigade was the advance. We went in with over 800 men in the regiment. There came out but 216, all told, unhurt.[8]

Some "ball" at Gettysburg! And in defiance of Commanding General Lee's order *not* to shoot first and bring on a general battle. His order was reiterated specifically by Corps Commander A.P. Hill to Brigadier General Henry Heth.[9] It turned out Heth's small-scale beginning had the nastiest unintended consequence: defeat.

Lee's plan failed at the beginning of Day One, not on the last day at the Charge up to the Angle, with disobedience of his orders. Little men like to shoot big guns.

The ruination of his *"wisest, grandest, most imposing scheme"* started near Willoughby Run, west of Gettysburg on the Chambersburg Pike before Lee knew it.

His plan should not have failed—except for two presidents.

President Jefferson Davis had not agreed with his field commander to set up the "army in effigy" near Washington. Lee wanted to, needed to, fake Lincoln's army out of position and keep it in place near Washington rather than in pursuit of his army. Had the Northern Army of the Potomac drawn back to protect Washington, D.C. from Beauregard's "army in effigy," Lee could have ranged freely to the banks of the Susquehanna. He could have made his peace proclamation to counteract the six-months-old Emancipation Proclamation, then quickly returned to Virginia with thousands more than 60,000 head of Pennsylvania farm animals.

President Abraham Lincoln, on the other hand, as Commander-in-Chief had ordered his army to do what it had not done previously: Lee's army was the objective. According to Honest Abe it would not be the defense of Washington nor the capture of Richmond which would seal the end of the conflict. Had the Southern Army of Northern Virginia not been followed by the Northern Army of the Potomac, it would not, could not have been defeated in Pennsylvania by the army *in absentia* in the soft underbelly of the North where there were few, so very few, military resources.

Lee admitted what happened to his plan at Gettysburg was his fault, all his fault. He was right. He should have stopped the invasion and stayed in Virginia when his Confederate president did not support him. Or, he should have returned from up north to Virginia unscathed when the Federal president's army appeared, rather than persisting in getting to York to enact his pacific plan. He should not have fought a general battle, *unless attacked.* Clearly both of Lee's metaphoric feet and toes, partly of iron and partly of clay, were shot off effectively by the accidental battle at Gettysburg.

Both chief executives interfered before R. E. Lee could get to York, eat Pennsylvania Dutch hogmaw with sausage, celery, cabbage, and potatoes, then "seven sweets and seven sours" subsequent to making his startling proclamation of peace from the court house on Continental Square.

Regardless of what happened, R. E. Lee retreated undoomed. Defeated, but not doomed.

Lee wouldn't acknowledge defeat at Gettysburg, virtually sizing it up as a favorable result. Historian Gary Gallagher notes that shortly after the battle, Lee "told an officer that Federals had suffered such damage at Gettysburg that 'it will be seen for the next six months that *that* army will be as quiet as a sucking dove.'"[10]

A sucking dove is a strange image for a keenly rational engineer under normal circumstances, but as a frustrated peace-seeker he was an irrational strategist given to strange thoughts. Lee should have been thinking judiciously about getting his troops home safely *before* the accidental conflict at Gettysburg. Nor was he astute and sagacious during the battle. After the battle the rain must have cleared his senses and the retreat sharpened his military instincts so that Gettysburg was not a debacle collapsing his army into the flooding Potomac.

When one remembers that Lee's "sickness" at Gettysburg was psychosomatic in nature, one realizes that such a condition does not miraculously cease in negative situations such as a retreat. The continuing severity of the rainfall, the flooded river blocking his army's passage across the Potomac into Virginia, and Meade's hovering army each and all three must have plagued him constantly until he got back into Virginia.

He was sinking into magical thinking, notoriously an irrational act, and he didn't recognize it. The phrase "sucking doves" doesn't befit a commanding general of an army that had thousands of its best slaughtered while he sat watching from a log on Seminary Ridge the third day at Gettysburg—watching 13,000 men march almost a mile in full view of their enemy then charge uphill to be slaughtered.

In Autumn 1863, by accounts, Lee was thinking of invading the North a third time:

SEPTEMBER 4th.—There is a rumor that Gen. Lee (who is still here) is to take the most of his army out of Virginia, [to go southward or westward] to recapture the Southern territory lost by Loring, Pemberton, and Bragg. I doubt this; for it might involve the loss of Richmond, and indeed of the whole State of Virginia. … It may be, however, that this is a ruse, if so, Lee is preparing for another northern campaign.[1]

[OCTOBER 2nd] It is now said that Gen. Lee, despairing of being attacked in his chosen position, has resolved to attack Meade, or at least to advance somewhere. It is possible … that he will cross the Potomac again—at least on a foraging expedition. If he meets with only conscripts and militia he may penetrate as far as Harrisburg.[12]

In not acknowledging defeat there lies a self-placed booby-trap: one could catch oneself as the unwary quarry. To deny that one is defeated when the facts-on-the-ground show otherwise is the worst thing to do with an already defective and unfavorable situation. Lee must have been thinking he had the best looking boat … at the bottom of the sea. Even saying, "defeat isn't bitter if you don't swallow it," while in a bad situation, delivers a skunky taste from the glob in the mouth. Recovery, then, is made all the more difficult; restoration of élan becomes time-consuming and is chancy at best.

Wars are won and lost by emotions. More wars, however, are lost by emotions than are won. Some wars are lost because battles are lost by mislaid emotions, emotions put in the wrong place or at the wrong time. Gettysburg is a prime example. Lee's statement to Longstreet that "the enemy is there and that's where we will fight" is one of obscuring emotion because it states only one's specific condition and does not take into clear account the enemy's specific condition. Troubles ensue from emotions; big emotions cause big troubles on battlefields where cool heads with firm strategies and solid tactics are needed.

Thence General Lee exacerbated the situation by making another emotional statement after the Charge to the Angle: "It's all my fault. *You must help me*." That terrible demand from one who is to be the competent decision-maker for tens of thousands of men is impudence. It may sound humble and cause people to think he was self-deprecating, but the statement indicates one who is not in rational command of his faculties. It tells of one who wants others to bear still another burden that will cause them to sacrifice again, and die like those remaining on the battlefield. Lee was awfully "out of it" for days before the battle, since he realized his peace proclamation was totally compromised. Stymied at Gettysburg, Lee knew he could not go any farther, win or lose.

Thus it was that Robert E. Lee forced himself to fight almost two more years. He won some, lost others, often. Still, he was not doomed personally, militarily, nor politically; his *virtus,* manly excellence, prevented such a severe judgment. Others paid for that *virtus.*

꙳꙳꙳

After the war, as president of a struggling college with its demanding duties—enrollments, academics, staffing, finances, depleted physical plant, public relations—Lee had minimal time to appraise defeat in war or to examine his denial of defeat. Then, when exhaustion took hold in 1870, recommendations for an extended vacation made sense to him. He left Lexington for a purpose-driven tour of four states, then a return home. During that trip R. E. Lee discovered a reality greater than his life, greater than the South, greater than a massive war to settle a political problem and social evil.

In the last year of his life he discovered what he wrestled with since the war's end. There is a reward greater than tasks performed dutifully, whether in a victorious or a defeated military career.

The reward? Understanding that if winning is the only thing in the world of ultimate importance then there's a weakness in the soul that needs to be faced—and overcome. That understanding is wisdom, the pearl of great price. Neither victory nor defeat is finally important; what matters is how a human being handles either of them. Or both of them.

Evidence of the discovery of something greater was inadvertent, spontaneous, physically demanding, but touching. It was quite real— with significance for the remaining months of his human existence. Lee's discovery, and that evidence, hinged on his health.

Early in 1870 three of Washington College's faculty, former military colleagues, had noticed Lee's diminishing health. They'd urged him to take an extended vacation; he resisted, as expected. Several Lexington physicians also agreed he should vacation and convinced him to accept, suggesting travel southward to a warmer environment where he had not been since early in the war years, almost a decade before.

Shortly thereafter he appointed the professor of philosophy as acting president of Washington College. As well, he turned care of his wife over to their daughter Mary, who was visiting at the time, and to their son Custis, who was teaching at VMI across the road from WC. Then he took their daughter Agnes—or she took him—on a trip from the mountains of western Virginia heading southeast to the seashore area of Savannah, Georgia.

Leaving Lexington by coach to the river landing for a canal boat, he was greeted by faculty members and hundreds of his college students at the dock. This event foreshadowed the remainder of his trip, but father and daughter did not realize it. The dockside throng brought exactly what he didn't want: public attention.

The canal trip to Richmond resulted in a trio of big city physicians examining him to confirm or give thumbs down to their backcountry colleagues' suggestion for a traveling vacation southward. Lee passed muster.

While in Richmond he met together with former colonel John Mosby, the famous—or infamous—"Gray Ghost" Confederate cavalry guerilla fighter, and with former general George Pickett, whose division was decimated in the Charge to the Angle at Gettysburg. Before meeting with Lee, Picket told Mosby that he "would pay his respects to the general [Lee] but did *not* want to be alone with him!"[13] Pickett was disturbed that he might be uncivil for how Lee had botched the battle on the third day at Gettysburg.

The meeting with Mosby was cordial, yet the "Gray Ghost" found Lee terribly 'oppressed by the great memories' and *pacifist* in his conversation, [As he had] *repudiated* war to nephew Edward Childe and a Washington College patron, …." [14] The discovery amazed Mosby; like so many others he did not really know Robert E. Lee.

The meeting with Pickett was chilly; it dropped to freezing quickly. On both their parts. Picket regretted attending the meeting as much as he regretted his own unwillingness to dispute his former commander.

Upon leaving the hotel room, "Pickett burst out bitterly against Lee, calling him 'that old man,' and saying, 'He had my division *slaughtered* at Gettysburg.'"[15]

War can make friends enemies; *vice versa*, also.

Strikingly, Robert E. Lee's pacifism became more evident than in Mosby's declaration. In fact, Lee "kept away purposely from the places that revived the memory of the war … wherever he traveled."[16] It was a continuation of his choice ever since the end of the war. "On horseback he never rode over any of the fields where his troops had been engaged. … All this was deliberate. Had he been able to do so he would have ploughed up the trenches and would have followed the example he applauded 'of those nations [that] endeavored to obliterate the marks of civil strife.'"[17] Robert E. Lee became Beowulf: the "battle sick one."[18]

Robert E. Lee had seen too much blood spilled, too many brains splattered, too much humanity destroyed on battlefields. He had smelled so much revolting gas from decomposing bodies, he had tasted way too much cabbage meal after meal after meal, he had touched so much trembling horse flesh, so many human bodies quaking under fire that he could no longer fathom war.

On top of which he had heard manifold lies declared to be truth and spoken as if they were the very words of creation. Lies and cant, falsehoods and sanctimony were often speechified vociferously by hotheaded extremists. Few of them ever put their bodies on the line, yet they rationalized killing corporeal human beings for abstract social or political theories. So often he had witnessed the *imago Dei* devoured in honest men, countless noble men, wolfed down in war's hell—that he *repudiated* war. War was wrong categorically. R. E. Lee rejected war as a way for human beings to treat other human beings.

Officially there isn't such a being as "Lee the Peace Seeker." We've been acclimated to Lee the War Maker, though that title does not describe the human being he actually became. And some people want to bury the full human being he became, even though he had told his comrades-in-arms he wasted his life in the military. Such people want to save their idea of Robert Edward Lee. But the idea of Robert Edward Lee and the man Robert Edward Lee are two distinct entities. People carve him in stone on a mountain or cast him in bronze on a statue or sculpt him in marble on a catafalque, but he is none of those representations. His words tell the R. E. Lee he became. Those words bespeak the very crown of his life.

He has suffered such a thin fate. Usually portrayed in military uniform and often on horseback, Robert Lee is so represented because it is easily done. As a peace-seeker he is as difficult to illustrate as is peace itself. War and warriors are spectacular and simply shown as such. Peace, differently, is neither sensational nor bombastic and takes spiritual depth as well as physical skill to portray. Robert Lee needs an additional layer added to his representations, similar to an Abraham Lincoln seated determinedly in a pavilion or a Thomas Jefferson standing firm in a rotunda or even a Winston Churchill with a raised arm in victory as is located in Washington, D.C. at the British Embassy.

But in 1870 he was on a personal mission, and it did not include formal declarations of pacifism. R. E. Lee was neither propagandist nor evangelist; he was a warrior reborn as a human being seeking personal peace for himself, for his ruptured state, and for his country reunited.

Father and daughter continued the vacation trip where he could get away from the war that had ended five years before. The trip could revive him to finish what might well be his last year at Washington College now that it was on solid footing. Then he could retire. With family and solitude around him, he would retire to a farm. Always a farm. Everyone has a place, a piece of land in his or her head. A farm fills that need admirably.

While in Richmond, father and daughter realized the responsibility for trip necessities was so demanding that daughter Agnes needed help managing their affairs. Out of the blue, Lee's former chief supply officer, James Corley, volunteered to accompany them. Corley willingly would supervise the ordinary and extraordinary chores associated with travel arrangements. His offer was a boon appreciated from the bottom of their hearts and soles of their feet, by both father and daughter. That kindness foreshadowed again what would occur throughout the trip—and Lee didn't want—public generosity.

The small party headed south to Warrenton, North Carolina, near the Virginia border, to a remote cemetery. Arriving by train at night, Lee was immediately recognized by a veteran who invited them to his home for lodging. After breakfast the next day the host provided the carriage and directions while the hostess gave Agnes white hyacinths for the grave.

For the first and last time Robert E. Lee visited the grave of his second daughter. Named Anna for Lee's mother she was "precious Annie" to him, so close to his heart because she understood him so well. When she was young he called her "Little Raspberry." Yet she had died at age 23, from typhoid, a sickness that stems from the bacterium *Salmonella*. As a father, part of his emotional heart died, too, during the war and he considered her a casualty among the other war dead. He knew the view of ancient Greek historian Herodotus, that in peace children bury their fathers, in war fathers bury their children. A daughter gone, but his heart held firm amidst the tears.

Years before Annie's father and her sister Agnes had visited her grave, the local citizens, out of love for Lee, had raised money and erected a tall gravestone in Annie's memory. He was at war, and could only be thankful for their Charity beyond charity. He could not help but be moved by the generosity of people who knew little about "precious Annie." They kept her memory alive, caring for the gravesite, waiting, as it were, for her precious father. What can a father say to people who act so deeply out of love for him that they love a daughter's memory, too? The mystery of love has no answer—and need never be asked, only appreciated and reciprocated.

R. E. Lee was beginning to feel a spirit moving in his heart. The care he had encountered during the first weeks of travel since leaving Lexington began to mark him.

The party left the Warren Plains train station for Georgia. The train, however, was preceded by something more rapid: a telegraph message. At Raleigh, North Carolina *"General Lee is aboard"* spread throughout the city and citizens poured out of their homes in the darkness to await the train and their beloved general.

What happened in North Carolina was the beginning of a series of similar episodes that would take place all along the railroad line. At crossroads, in hamlets and towns, even in the countryside people lined the tracks to view the train he was on. Telegrams whizzed over the wires, spontaneous gatherings and planned assemblies, small groups in small towns, large crowds in large towns, bands played and bands of brothers in arms stood at attention to greet him, multitudes of children, youth, adults gathered. Even babes in arms were held high to view him so parents could tell them later in life, "You saw General Lee!"

Lee wanted no such acclaim, no such honoring; it belonged to the men who served with him and those who died for a cause. He knew the truth. Love and praise were more than he expected; they belonged elsewhere.

The overwhelming feelings kept surging mile-by-mile among ordinary people; something else was surging within him. His rational appreciation for the gratitude and respect was beginning to bend under the admiration and compassion by all the people along the way. He had never heard of such love for a defeated leader. Nor did anyone else ever know of such abiding respect for a loser.

He was conflicted; the crowds touched his heart but his heart was with those men who served while sometimes starving, often shoeless, and those who had died needing neither food nor garment. All the homes with empty beds, broken hearts, vacant chairs, fatherless children, and nowhere to turn for help, softened his bleeding heart. In most every place, the multiple places, the only thing he could do was raise his hat in salute.

No speeches, no words, not even gratitude. He was overwhelmed, literally. The love Robert Lee felt filled him with emotion so overpowering he could not respond verbally.

Seldom did he say a word. He was the word. The people heard him, clearly.

It was a mystery. No one attempted to solve it. It was becoming evident that life, even death, are not problems to be solved like a school child's arithmetic drills. Life, death and love are mysteries to be grateful for, to be enjoyed for what they present to human beings. In place after place after place, including the open country along the train tracks, they gathered for one man, one human being who had lived and served dutifully.

Through South Carolina into Georgia the crowds enlarged, praise increased. The people wanted to see, to hold in their hearts the dutiful man, the defeated general who was not beaten down or beaten up, the quiet college president who was helping prepare young men for a new day in the South, in America. Those college students needed a leader, not on horseback to fight, but one who would help them adjust to life beyond defeat—just as he had adjusted by taking a humble position, that of helping others and making the most of a poor situation. He wanted the present generation to overcome loss—and coming generations to prevent losses.

Savannah was thronged with the largest crowd ever assembled there, to that time. However, the experience with friends from before the war and early in it—when he had been there to build its defenses—was of greater value than the press of thousands. Too, individual friends from West Point years filled his time. Former classmate and fellow general Joseph E. Johnston filled his heart. A photographer took their picture: two enwisened men, bearing the weight of war, the millstone of countless deaths, the albatross of defeat—not upon shoulders but in their hearts. They talked quietly, conscious it was the last time they would see one another. Meeting again in old age a friend with whom one has suffered, is to share riches that can't be stolen because they're way too heavy with caring, and love, and respect to carry away.

Then, on to Cumberland Island off the coast of Georgia, to visit again his father's grave. "Light-Horse Harry" Lee had tried to get home back in 1818 from his five-year self-imposed exile in the Caribbean. The demeaning exile was the result of longstanding financial debacles from land speculation, not all his fault; of constant marital infidelities, all his fault; and of severe physical problems brought on by the horrible and unwarranted beating he had suffered in July 1812 while visiting a friend who was a newspaper editor opposed to the War of 1812.

The years in the Caribbean left Henry Lee woefully heartsick, piteously lonely. He became seriously ill, sailed on a vessel returning to the States and requested the captain—whom he had badgered to secure passage to America—to disembark him on an island near Savannah, Georgia. The daughter of his former commander, long dead General Nathaneal Greene of the Revolutionary War, took him in. She nursed him for several weeks before he died. Friends buried him on the barrier island named Cumberland. Never to see family in Virginia again, nor good enough to serve the United States of America again, "Light-horse Harry" passed, falling short of returning to a wife who loved him and a son who still waited for a father.

Over the years, visits to his father's gravesite were always of unresolved value for Robert Lee. This last one was, too, with a daughter—his father's granddaughter—along. He had always loved his father; he was conflicted, though, about his sire's own conflicted life. Daughter Agnes was an excellent companion on the trip; she had never known her grandfather but she knew how to steady his son, bringing the comfort of family love to R. E. Lee's still-struggling soul.

They left Georgia for a vacation-within-a-vacation in close by northeastern Florida. For the first time R. E. Lee ate oranges fresh from the tree. A small pleasure but sweet as he tasted the kindness of Floridians in their sweet oranges. The excursion into Florida was helpful, yet when the boat left the crowds at the docks stood silent. Silence for the first time on the trip! Everywhere else cheering, but in Florida ------------- silence! As was said by an ancient psalmist: "They looked upon him and were radiant!" What need for sound? They had seen the word.

Back up in Savannah physicians examined him again. He passed muster, or so they said. During the visit he received invitations to visit places far inland, as distant as Kentucky. One would think he was on the American version of the "Grand Tour" of the European continent.

They proceeded to South Carolina along the Atlantic coast then into North Carolina with receptions the same as occurred on the southward leg of his trip. Good news about a good man travels as fast as the purported speed of bad news. People just kept coming to see an old man raise his hat in the salute of appreciation. And they cheered. He melted, but wanted no more.

Finally the party entered the Old Dominion. Lee met his wartime confidential assistant, Walter Taylor, a noble alter ego who devotedly and warmly had performed that role to ease his stresses. Another old friend makes old age agreeable, at least for a time.

Virginia filled the air with rockets, cannon, and cheers as if R. E. Lee were Julius Caesar home from a campaign or Alexander the Great setting off on one.

It was a bit much for a simple college president. On Sunday the streets were filled with dignified church-goers who out of their respect for the holiness of the day did not make noise nor cheer, nonetheless every head was bared, many eyes flowed with tears as he proceeded to Christ Church for services. Men who had served Old Virginy stood ramrod erect, saluted a commander who had no rank and no army, but continued to do his duty as he saw it.

Back again in his home state where he gave up so much to serve in war, Lee was as disquieted as he had been elsewhere on the journey. The unsolicited acclamation he received on his "vacation" was more than he thought proper. Absolutely more than he thought he deserved.

What he received was reverent respect. People beheld a human leader courageous to the end though defeated time and again. On the other hand he felt sequestered in an airy, insubstantial condition, unworthy of attention, and incapable of doing more than directing the education of young men for another year to a future worthy of their forbears as Christian gentlemen.

The crowds and individuals who lined his way unknowingly created and merged their minute particles of reverent respect into an awe-inspiring nugget of historical gold that tells us so much about R. E. Lee. It was not military victories nor secessionism which caused people to care so fervently, so deeply for him—as final defeat was their end and Union their strength. The man himself was gold, superlatively more important than his partly iron, partly clay feet.

It is not true that one "can never ever overdo a good thing." Unlimited sugar becomes sickening; sunlight all the time begins a desert. Moderation is the good thing; moderation in *all* things is the best thing. Therefore, glad to be out of so much limelight and on the last leg of the two-months-long trip, father R. E. and daughter Agnes met wife and mother, Mary Custis Lee, at the home of son and brother William Henry Fitzhugh Lee.

"Rooney" had a farm. "E I, E I, O," how wonderful! And on the shore of the Pamunky! A river with a cheery, appealing sound for an old man who had had to cross many battlefield rivers like the Styx, glum and hostile from the afterworld of the ancient Greeks, hoping finally to get to the River Lethe of forgetfulness and oblivion ever more.

And Lee's namesake, Robert E. Lee, Jr., lived close by on another farm—double the joy for the father. The elder Lee, however, did verbally joust with Rob that he didn't take the best of care of his house, noting in a parental fashion that being an author is a valid reason—by a whisker.

Robert Edward Lee for most of his life had desired to be on a farm for the sensible life. Especially after the war, a farm would be Nature at work and Nature at rest, at the same time. A farm would be an unrivaled place, not only in Virginia, nor America, nor the world, but smack-dab in the hub of God's great Creation and everything would turn around it.

Rooney's farm, therefore, was a fitting conclusion to the southward trip. The elder Lee was gratified that the public segment was over, crowds gone, praise muted, sights seen, and respects paid. His health not damaged. Or so it seemed.

But he was tired. Saturday, 28 May 1870 they returned to the President's House at Washington College in Lexington. It had been over two months of vacation, preparatory to the autumn semester. He would begin the 1870-71 college year. He would not complete it.

Interesting to note, sixteen years after R. E. Lee's tour, the former Confederate president Jefferson Davis, in 1886 and 1887, also toured the South. Lee's tour had turned into a spontaneous and unrestrained triumphal passage gifted by Southern people for a man who led their brothers, husbands, fathers, sons in war to gain peace.

Davis' tour was planned; it was staged to justify Secession. He castigated the United States of America for interfering in United States business. Business with its constitute states, that is.

Davis didn't see a certain truth after the war any more than he saw it during the war. Then Lincoln had the necessity to deal with his individual states from the position of power inherent in a central government.

On various occasions Jefferson Davis had to deal with his individual states from a position of power inherent in a central government during the days of the Confederacy. Individuals and states had castigated him, severely, some wanting to secede from the Confederate Secession. The Confederate Congress disliked him as much as he disliked it, as it tried, none too well, to do its business, as elected to do it. Blind in an eye, Davis was also blind in a political dimension.

Greeted on his tour, Jefferson Davis also heard cheers. He, too, received approval. He, too, had led their brothers, husbands, fathers, sons to defeat as they tried to destroy the United States of America by splitting the states asunder. His purpose failed in war. It failed in political thought and action over and again, but lingers into the twenty-first century. It is almost the case that carved on tablets of granite in our minds, we human beings love our failings well. It is so strong a case that one would think our failings come from the hormones in our self-stimulating loins rather than from our clever minds that can operate duplicitously about issues, at one and the same time on both sides of an issue, like a lawyer. Davis' mistake became Davis' life after the war; he hung on it for he had little else since he never won a battle.

It is to his discredit that he enfleshed the concept of the Confederacy as The Lost Cause. As has been noted since his time, more Americans than not view it as "a cultural illusion without equal."[19] Jefferson Davis became a clanging cymbal for a dead cause.

Robert Edward Lee became the soul of the South.

It is clear that on the trip R. E. Lee was seeking solace about his health condition. Knowing his history one can imagine without fear of exaggeration he was also seeking solace for his soul, given his mature religious experience at forty-six years of age.

Most assuredly that solace he sought was about what the four-year-long fratricidal war had done to the people of the United States of America who, too, were seeking solace from that benighted war. It had almost destroyed the Perpetual Union and would have ruined both "nations" had it gone Jefferson Davis' way with the Confederate cause.

Robert Lee's 1870 searching was not chiefly about the pain caused by a bad war over a bad issue. The search was about his own understanding of the continual love—way beyond adulation—from the thousands of people all along the way of his trip. Those people had suffered tremendous losses for his and others' leadership in that war, for whatever reason they, personally or collectively, had.

That personal search underlying all the ongoing phenomena of meetings, gatherings, and events he encountered was faced with love unbounded all along the way. It was freely given to Robert Lee when he least expected anything. The people had a love that would not let him go unwanted, uncared for, though his misguided war efforts had cost them their fathers, sons, brothers, husbands, sometimes their all. How could Lee grasp and then respond to such massive human endowment by ordinary Southerners five years after the war, still struggling through defeat and destruction, death and damnation?

His intellectual understanding must have broken under the pure glory of love freely given—though all his military efforts equaled zero.

The former general who wanted no more to do with war doubtless realized that had the South won the war he would have lost his soul!

Transformation came to the soul of the South in a manner never imagined by South or North: Lee, the defeated, was revered as indestructible, undoomed.

Robert Edward Lee had been shadowed, enshrouded from early childhood. The shadow was transformed twenty-three years *after* the freakish shooting incident during the Mexican War. The cause of the illumination was his vacation trip, a spontaneously bestowed triumphal tour. The public demonstrations in 1870 poured out reverence; they confirmed he was undoomed again, as when shot at from point blank range by an American soldier in 1847.

That undoomed condition still exists for R. E. Lee. It comes down to Americans in the present, a fantastic condition that has persisted for over a century and a half. He is not thought of as traitor. The American public does not consider him a failure, contrary to the military evidence. The America public—not only Southerners—holds him above hero status, far above most American presidents.

The man was not doomed in his lifetime. He did not succeed in his plan for peace. All battles lost on one hand and on the other his unfulfilled wise, grand, and imposing plan for peace—neither or both had doomed him in the four years of the war.

Nor is he doomed today. He remains undoomed, not because of monuments erected or carved, honors or speeches given. Riverboats and trains popularly named for him can't doom him either, for if defeat couldn't ruin him, "success" can't either.

He is undoomed today because he has the respect and reverence of people for his *duty to obey duties*. Duties to self, duties to others, duties to homeland, duties to God—all these long decades since he died—have saved him for us.

A precious particle of human gold has come down to us in the person of Robert Lee, contrary to our misperception that he was as faultless a human being as he was a military cadet at West Point.

R. E. Lee was gold, with partly iron and partly clay mixed in to endure through time.

The same today: an undoomed warrior in war, an undoomed seeker for peace.

Chapter Notes

1. Walter Nugent. Habits of Empire: A History of American Expansion (N.Y.: Knopf, 2008): 187.
2. E. A. Hitchcock. Fifty Years in Camp and Field. W. A. Croffut,. Ed. (N. Y.: Putnam's. 1901): 201-2.
3. Will Durant's actual quote is "We are what we repeatedly do. Excellence, then, is not an act, but a habit." See: Will Durant. The Story of Philosophy (N.Y.: Simon and Shuster, 1926): Durant's quote is misattributed to Aristotle.
4. Elizabeth Brown Pryor. Reading the Man (N. Y.: Viking, 2007): 231.
5. Ibid.

6.   Edward L. Childe. Life and Campaigns of General Lee. George Litting, Trans. (London: Chatto and Windus, 1875):187.

7.   Holy Bible (AV). Daniel chap. 2. For the full story, see specifically verses 31-43. (Emphases added)

8.   WR/OR. I. 27.2. 645. (Emphasis added)

9.   Benedict R. Maryniak. "Gettysburg's First Shot" at website http://www.gdg.org/Research/Authored%20Items/arshot.html

10. David and Jeanne Heidler (eds.) Encyclopedia of the American Civil War: A Political, Social, and Military History (N.Y.: Norton, 2000): 1160.

11. John Beauchamp Jones. A Rebel War Clerk's Diary (Phila.: Lippincott, 1866): Vol. II, Chp. 30. 32. (Emphasis added)

12. Ibid. Vol. II, chap. 31. 60.

13. Charles R. Flood. Lee: The Last Years (Boston: Houghton Mifflin Mariner Book, 1998): 231.

14. E. B. Pryor. op. cit. 457. (Emphases added)

15. C. R. Flood. op cit. 232. (Emphasis added)

16. Douglas Southal Freeman. R .E. Lee:A Biography. Vol. 4. (N.Y.: Scribner's, 1934): 455.

17. Ibid., Vol. 4. chap. 25. 456.

18. David Breeden. The Adventures of Beowulf (London: Watkins Publishing, 2011): Line 3063.

19. Everett Carter. "Cultural History Written With Lightning: The Significance of The Birth of a Nation," American Quarterly. Fall 1960. 355.

CPSIA information can be obtained at www.ICGtesting.com
Printed in the USA
BVOW012317060613

322659BV00006B/9/P